The
East African
Mounted Rifles

The
East African
Mounted Rifles

Experiences of the Campaign in the
East African Bush During the
First World War

C J Wilson

LEONAUR

The East African Mounted Rifles: Experiences of the Campaign in the East African Bush During the First World War

Originally published circa 1938 under the title *The Story of the East African Mounted Rifles*

Published by Leonaur Ltd

Material original to this edition and its origination in this form copyright © 2006 Leonaur Ltd

ISBN (10 digit): 1-84677-059-9 (hardcover)
ISBN (13 digit): 978-1-84677-059-3 (hardcover)

ISBN (10 digit): 1-84677-042-4 (softcover)
ISBN (13 digit): 978-1-84677-042-5 (softcover)

http://www.leonaur.com

Publishers Notes

In the interests of authenticity, the spellings, grammar and place names used in this book have been retained from the original edition.

The opinions of the author represent a view of events in which he was a participant related from his own perspective; as such the text is relevant as an historical document.

The views expressed in this book are not necessarily those of the publisher.

Contents

Appendices

List of Illustrations

Chapter One
Early Days in Nairobi

August 4th, 1914, found British East Africa in general, and Nairobi, its capital, in particular, in a state of expectant excitement and confused activity. The news of the declaration of war with Germany had got everybody guessing as to the probable course of events in East Africa. There were those who said that hostilities would be confined to Europe, and that war between two white races in a black man's country was unthinkable; there were others who hoped for an immediate advance on Tabora, and the speedy conquest of German East Africa; while others again anticipated an attack on Nairobi by overwhelming enemy forces.

There was a rush of volunteers, clamouring to be enlisted; but the reception they received was not at first altogether encouraging. As a matter of fact nobody knew what to do, since there was no organised machinery for dealing with the situation, and for a while all was confusion. For instance, the declaration of war was announced at Eldoret during a meeting which had been called to discuss some agricultural subject; forthwith ensued a wild ride by the settlers from the Plateau, on horse or mule, some riding bareback, all bound for Nairobi. After a desperate ride through the night, down the seventy miles of atrocious road to Londiani, and the tedious railway journey from there onwards, this eager band of volunteers met, so it is said, with rather a chilly reception on their arrival in Nairobi.

There was a feeling abroad in certain quarters that there would be "nothing doing." However there was something doing, and once it began everybody seemed to be doing it at the same time, and in his own way. There were as many volunteer corps coming into existence as there were rooms in Nairobi House, which had become the Volunteer Forces Headquarters.

At last order grew out of chaos, and the East African Mounted Rifles came into being, as the one recognized corps of mounted volunteers. Into it were absorbed all those separate collections of volunteers which were gallantly endeavouring to organize themselves independently. Such were Bowker's Horse, the Plateau South Africans, the Legion of Frontiersmen, Wessel's Scouts, and others.

Of these separate units, Bowker's Horse strove hard to retain its individuality; but in the end better counsels prevailed. The number of mounted men available was all too small, and it was essential that they should be combined as one regiment. This concession was made to the gallant leader, Russell Bowker, that his men, while wearing "E.A.M.R." on their shoulder straps, should be allowed to retain the letters "B.H." on their helmets.

The East African Mounted Rifles, as now formed, consisted of six squadrons, a maxim gun section, and signallers. Later there was added a special section of Scouts. Captain H. H. Sandbach, late of the 1st Royal Dragoons, was appointed Commanding Officer, with Major H. S. Laverton, late of the 3rd Hussars, second in command. Captain C. M. Taylor, late R.F.A., was appointed Adjutant. The Squadron Commanders were Captains A. K. O'Brien, Russell Bowker, P. Chapman, A. F. Arnoldi, A. E. Bingley, and M. H. Wessels. Last, but by no means least, must be mentioned the Regimental Sergeant-Major, J. MacNab Mundell, late of the 9th Lancers.

It is impossible to say how much the E.A.M.R., in those early days, owed to the Adjutant and the Regimental Sergeant-Major, for their devoted exertions in the face of the most heart-breaking difficulties. They were faced with the problem of creating a regiment out of raw material which, however excellent in its composition, was mostly quite undisciplined and untrained. This superhuman task had to be completed within a period not of months or even several weeks but within a few days.

It is equally difficult to appreciate at its full value the work which was done by the Quartermaster, Lieutenant J. W. Milligan, who was called upon to equip the rapidly growing regiment with all the thousand-and-one items of supply and equipment. It was a colossal effort to find and provide supplies from everywhere, and to furnish equipment from nowhere; for, of course, there was no already established military store or depot from which to draw. In this work the Quartermaster had the invaluable assistance of the Regimental Quartermaster-Sergeant, H. F. Murrell, and Squadron Quartermaster-Sergeant J. J. Scally.

Regimental Headquarters remained at Nairobi House, but a camp was formed at the Race Course. Here, under the kindly care of Lieut. the Hon. A. Bailey, Troop Leader of "C" Squadron, the varied assortment of recruits began to fall into shape and "muck in together". It was not made compulsory for officers or men to live in camp. Those who were residents of Nairobi continued to live at home, while others were allowed to stay in hotels and clubs. This freedom from restriction was all very well in its way, but was scarcely the ideal method for promoting habits of discipline, or for encouraging camaraderie and *esprit de corps.*

The different squadrons used to choose their own times and places for drilling. "A" Squadron used to parade in the neighbourhood of the Norfolk Hotel. At this time one troop of "A" Squadron was armed with the lance, in addition to the rifle. There was an idea that in the approaching campaign a troop of lancers would be of great utility in slaying large numbers of the enemy, the enemy presumably being imagined as continually on the run. The lances were only pig-spears, and it cannot be said that "Monica's Own" ever attained to the highest degree of efficiency with these weapons, for all their assiduous practice. It is to be recorded with thankfulness that in spite of the most desperate feats, entirely unintentional, not one of these gallant lancers succeeded in impaling himself, his horse, or his comrade. Their lances, alas, were never blooded on the field of battle. They were soon discarded, to the sorrow of the Squadron Commander, but to the relief and safety of the troopers.

Other squadrons carried out their parades and drills in the vicinity of the Race Course. On one occasion a certain squadron set forth from camp for the first time for real battle practice, complete with blank ammunition. The correct procedure in mounted infantry fighting was duly followed: one man in every four was left to hold the mules, the others ran forward and blazed away in "rapid independent". Splendid! Until came the order to retire and mount, when all that could be seen of their mounts was a distant cloud of dust towards the Race Course, whither the mules had decided to bolt, at the first burst of firing. It was a crest-fallen Squadron that tramped back on foot, to face the ill-timed jests of their friends.

The mule may have been created for some good purpose, but as a substitute for a warhorse he can best be described as matter out of place. All the horses that could be found had been commandeered for the E.A.M.R., but there were not nearly enough to go round, and the deficiency was made up with mules. On parade and during drill they were the cause of much bitterness of spirit and blasphemy: on patrol and in action they were an absolute danger.

To dress a troop containing untrained horses and fractious mules into anything like military precision was a sheer impossibility. To try to get that troop into extended order, with every mule imbued with an innate determination to jam itself close against the nearest horse, was worse. But in justice to the mules it must be admitted that their powers of endurance were wonderful; however long the patrol or march, however great the disproportion between the hefty trooper and his tiny mount the little mule always came home literally full of buck.

If the provision of suitable mounts for the E.A.M.R. was a difficulty, the supply of arms and equipment was also a formidable problem. Many recruits had brought with them their own sporting rifles, of any and every calibre, with which they were ready to take the field; but fortunately it was found possible to gather together enough service .303 rifles, of a sort, to equip the Regiment throughout with these, thus at least simplifying the question of ammunition.

Not so much uniformity was attained in the matter of dress; in fact it may be said that the only "uniform" consisted of the letters "E.A.M.R.", borne on the shoulder straps. For the rest, each man wore that which was right in his own eyes, and dressed himself as fancy or the state of his wardrobe dictated. Headgear ranged from smart khaki helmets to the shabbiest and flabbiest "terai". Coats or tunics, if worn at all, usually had the sleeves cut off at the shoulders, and in time such a sleeveless tunic became practically uniform for Colonel and trooper alike, since it certainly was convenient. Lower down came riding-breeches, slacks, or shorts, according to taste: below these, gaiters or puttees. The tout ensemble might be completed by a gaily coloured scarf round the neck, and a feather in the hat.

An East African Mounted Rifleman on the warpath was a wonderful sight. Straddled across a diminutive mule, and slung around with rifle, bandoliers, haversack and waterbottle, with perhaps a bush-knife, revolver, field-glasses, and an odd billy-can or two as well, he resembled nothing so much as the White Knight of Alice's Adventures Through the Looking Glass.

By the middle of August it was agreed that equipment and training were far enough advanced for the E.A.M.R. to appear at a ceremonial parade. Accordingly a Grand Review was arranged on August 15th, at which the Governor and Commander-in-Chief, Sir Henry Conway Belfield, took the salute and inspected the Regiment. The Review passed off quite creditably, until our Commanding Officer unwisely called for "three cheers for His Excellency", when the sudden shout and wild waving of assorted headgear proved too much for the miserable mules, and the orderly ranks were promptly thrown into inextricable confusion.

Another military manoeuvre performed by the Regiment took the form of a trial railway journey. Men and animals entrained at Nairobi Station, and were conveyed four miles down the line. Here they were off-loaded, and then, repeating the motion, returned home. This exploit was carried out with the loss of only one mule.

As a further field exercise, towards the end of August, two squadrons and the maxim gun section were sent off from the Race Course, to live in camp about eight miles out along the Ngong Road. There they experienced for the first time the hardships of active service and the eccentricities of the Supply and Transport departments.

During that month of August there were many alarums and excursions in Nairobi. The air was full of rumours, and according to public opinion it was also full of German aeroplanes; at least they were constantly being reported, strangely enough always at night. Why an enemy aeroplane intending to fly over Nairobi, if such a thing had ever been at all possible, should always have chosen the night, and always have shown a bright light, has never been explained. As a matter of fact the only aeroplane which the Germans possessed, a machine brought out for the Exhibition at Dar es Salaam, is said to have crashed on its first flight.

One day a report was received that an aeroplane had been seen descending at Kijabe, as usual at night, and as usual showing a bright light. Of course Venus, the evening star, sets in the west, and Kijabe is west of Nairobi; but such a simple explanation of the mysterious light did not deter the "Powers That Be" from calling on the E.A.M.R. to furnish a patrol to proceed to Kijabe forthwith and capture the invader. However incredible, the fact remains that a mounted patrol of four men was despatched from Nairobi House that night, and fared forth along Sixth Avenue, bound for the heights of Kijabe on their quest of the mythical aeroplane.

Down the Uganda Railway, towards Voi, there was more happening. The Germans had opened the ball by capturing our frontier post, Taveta, which had been left without a garrison as being too isolated to be tenable. The defence of the Railway, in the Voi district, had been left to the King's African Rifles, the regular East African Native troops commanded by officers seconded from the British Army; but since it was thought that some sort of artillery would be useful, Lieut. F. H. de V. Joyce, then on the strength of the E.A.M.R., was put in charge of two antiquated Hotchkiss guns, and sent off with a detachment of ten men to see what could be done about it.

It was another part of the border, however, for which the Regiment was destined, and in the defence of which it was to play so large a part. In the light of subsequent events it was a significant incident when, on August 24th, Captain S. H. Charrington, with a party of signallers, departed for Mile 28 on the Magadi Railway, to co-operate with the Magadi Defence Force in the protection of that part of the border.

There were other detached parties of the E.A.M.R. sent off from Nairobi during August. Lieut. P. C. Joubert, of "D" Squadron, was despatched with a few picked men, on a special mission to the Dutch settlers around Arusha. A troop of "D" Squadron, under Sergt. J. H. Selby, set out for a long patrol of the German border in the Southern Masai Reserve. Corpl. H. Wreford Smith and two troopers of "C" Squadron left for Kajiado, and carried out a daring patrol as far as Meru Mountain. But it is impossible to follow in detail the adventures of special patrols such as these, since the history of them remains only in the memories of those who took part in them.

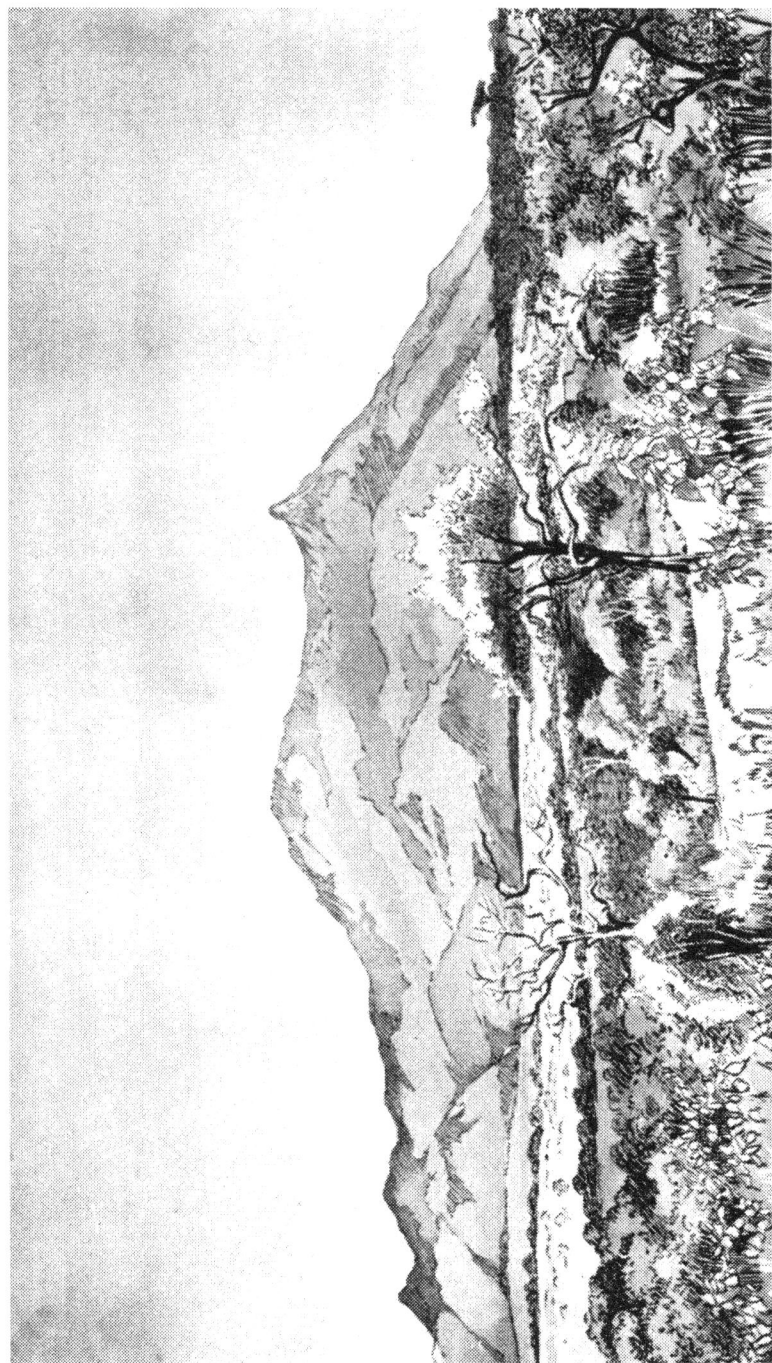

Longido Mountain.

A trooper.

Horse and Mule Patrol parading for inspection.

The Sergeants' Mess.
Back row: T. W. Patrick. J. M. Allen, L. Hawkins, H. C. Tryon, W. J. Evans,
C. M. Middleton, E Lloyd, R. Frederickson, C. A. Stradling, A. D. Impey, G.
Clothier, T. J. Noden, G. Q. Orchardson, F. Thorpe.
Middle row: A. Milne, A. H. Price, A. H. Gunnell, Capt. C. M. Taylor (Adjt.),
H. F. Murrell (R.Q.M.S.), Lt-Col. H. S. Laverton (C. O.), J. M. Mundell
(R.S.M.), L. J. Broom, W. E. George.
Front row: A. H. Colliver, E. M. V. Kenealy, G. Taylor.

Officers of the E.A.M.R. and E.A.V.C. inspecting remounts.

The officers and some men of "D" Squadron.

"D" Squadron leaving Longido to join the E.A.T.C.

Chapter Two
Guarding the Border

On August 30th things began to move in earnest. On that day news was received in Nairobi that a force of the enemy had crossed the border, and had reached Bissil River, less than twenty miles from Kajiado. Though this force, reported to consist of twenty Germans, could scarcely mean an attack on Nairobi, yet it was probably a serious attempt on either the main line of the Uganda Railway in the direction of Kiu, or on the Magadi Railway. Accordingly, orders were issued for "B" and "E" Squadrons to entrain immediately: "B" for Mile 28 on the Magadi Railway, and "E" for Kiu.

It was not to be the fortune of these two advance squadrons to meet the invading enemy; all the same they experienced to the full the hardships of East African campaigning. Of transport arrangements there were practically none. Each man carried what he could on his saddle; for the rest there was only such uncertain fare as the unappetizing kongoni.

"B" Squadron detrained at Kajiado, and forthwith took the field under that old and hardy campaigner, Russell Bowker. Accompanied by the Magadi Defence Force, which consisted of the employees of the Magadi Soda Company, they marched in the direction of the enemy.

During the course of the following day the Magadi Defence Force limped back to Kajiado, having tramped the twenty miles to Bissil and all the way back again, without having encountered the enemy. Meanwhile "B" Squadron pushed on beyond Bissil to Emombarasha, and then to Kedongai, where our scouts and signallers were.

"E" Squadron marched across country from Kiu to Emombarasha, followed "B" Squadron to Kedongai, and there the two squadrons joined forces on September 4th. At a camp at the base of Ol Doinyo Orok, only a few miles this side of the border, the Squadrons rested and waited for the arrival of stores, for man cannot live indefinitely on game alone, however plentiful.

The Squadrons then moved down to Namanga River, where they were joined by Lieut. Duirs and 18 men, who had been gathered in after the hurried departure from Nairobi and had followed on along the trail.

The adventures of Bowker's Horse during those days have been well described by J. G. Squiers, then a trooper in "B" Squadron, in a racy account of certain episodes connected with the E.A.M.R., under the title of "The Army that Found Itself", which appeared in serial form in the weekly journal East Africa. The story runs as follows:—

"We crawled into Kajiado at sunset, and had a meal of bread and bully, the last full meal we were to see for many a day. Next day we were to meet Hunger, and none who took any serious part in the East African campaign were ever out of sight of that bogey. Napoleon said 'An army marches on its stomach' I never met Napoleon, though I gather from his remark that he was in East Africa during the war. Anyway, he spoke a mouthful!

"Our first night march was a painful but illuminating experience. Ian Hay has noted the fact that; however slowly the front of a column may be moving at night, the tail is invariably running. As our horses were in front, the mule troop in rear was kept at an irregular and irritating jog-trot.

"We were loaded down with extra ammunition, horse feed, and various minor articles we had not learnt the art

of securing to our persons and saddles Consequently, the rear-guard became a kind of perambulating lost property office.

"There was no road, and we were led by two Masai guides in whom we placed little trust. We were not told how far we were going, what, if anything, we expected to meet, and how we were to act if we met it. We were in the heart of the Game Reserve, and kongoni snorted and herds of zebra yapped and stampeded round us and added to our tension and irritation.

"Every half minute somebody would pitch into a pig hole with a crash and a rattle. The two men behind him might avoid it, but the third generally found it again. We tried passing word down, and on a crash from the front the next two men would stage-whisper 'Hole' and the third man would get as far as 'Ho—!' before he found it. So we learnt to say 'Hole- right—left—or centre' ".

"Now and again a whistle would come out of the night. We would halt, and our Masai would answer and move forward. We huddled together in the bright moonlight until that weird whistle came again, when we pushed into the bush once more. We never saw the people who thus challenged us, and it was all very mysterious and thrilling, though what we were hankering after was information. Soon that changed to a simple desire for sleep and rest.

"On we went through patches of 'waitabit' thorn that tore clothes and flesh. Once when we were hung up in crossing a donga a rhino charged through the line and snorted off through the bush, while the squadron scattered for their lives. A few minutes later a man dropped asleep and fell from his saddle. His crazy mule charged through the ranks, somebody shouted 'rhino', and the now panicky column broke again. It was 1.30 a.m. before we finally halted at a small drift and ringed the animals for camp. We had ridden twenty-three miles on top of our train journey—not bad for our first day in the field.

"But our troubles had only started. There were pickets and horse guards to find, and hardly had my picket settled down than a hyena sneaked within twenty yards of us and laughed. There was a good deal of excuse for the hyena, but you can imagine the effect of that gibbering racket, at close range, on our over-strained nerves. Next, a rhino walked into a mounted picket and scattered them back through the camp. Lions put another picket up a tree, and then kept us lively with a concert of crashing roars until dawn.

"It was a very bleary-eyed, sleepy crew upon which the sun rose next morning. Then we found we had camped close to a supply dump for the I.D.* scouts, who had been standing to arms with rifles trained on us all night!

"It was surprising how soon we got familiar with such strange conditions. We got so used to prowling lions that the sentries simply threw stones and even boots in their direction. Hyenas developed a taste for tanned leather and often sneaked saddles from beneath the heads of sleeping men. Then the wrathy picket would follow the rattle of the stirrup irons until the brute let go its prize.

"From the I.D. dump we were issued with a pound of flour apiece, which we tied in our handkerchiefs or mixed in with the extra ammunition in our haversacks. Thus supplied, we rode into the bush once more. Our spirits had revived, and we were relying on capturing a German post to provide us with the next meal! Now it is difficult to look back and believe we were guilty of such insane optimism. It was to be a long time before we found a German post—or a meal.

"The average East African settler, not given to doing things for himself, knows about as much about cooking as a snake does of corsets. Imagine then, at the next halt, a hundred desperately hungry men, used to being waited on

---

* Intelligence Department

hand and foot, eighty per cent. of them without utensils of any kind, endeavouring to produce something edible from a handful of plain flour. Why, many hardly knew how to start a fire, or keep it alight. The average result looked like a species of volcanic lava, which, when broken open, revealed a loathsome, inedible grey paste.

"A few had had the foresight to provide themselves with mugs, billy cans, and perhaps a little coffee or salt, which things were soon at a premium and their owners remarkably popular. When we were at last convinced that there were no enemy in the immediate vicinity, a buck was shot, and we were issued with raw meat, about as useful to us as the flour; but we soon learnt what to do with it.

"When the flour gave out, we lived for several days on meat alone until a pack mule arrived with a little weevily rice. Tobacco and cigarettes were soon exhausted, but that was a minor hardship when there was so little to smoke on. My own cooking utensils were a 'Bushman's Friend' and an old Maconochie ration tin in which I cooked, and from which I ate everything I had for nearly a month. Any new Compulsory Service Scheme should include a course of cookery".

It was not long before the rest of the Regiment followed in the wake of these advance squadrons, for on September 7th a troop of "C" Squadron left Nairobi for Kajiado to prepare a camp, and the remainder were entrained in three troop trains the next day. By nightfall on that day the Regiment had bivouacked at Kajiado.

The next day was spent in pitching camp—a camp, however, which was not to be occupied for long. On September 10th two squadrons were warned to be in readiness to relieve "B" and "E" Squadrons, and their baggage carts were sent forward, under escort of a troop, to Orok. On September 11th, "A" and "F" Squadrons left for Bissil, while the C.O., with the Adjutant and the Squadron Commanders of "C" and "D", went forward on a ten days patrol, to reconnoitre the country between Kajiado and the border. On September 12th, "A" and "F" Squadrons had taken over charge of the forward posts from "B" and "E", "A" Squadron going forward to Kedongai, "F" remaining at Olekenoni Water on Emombarasha Mountain.

It was about this time that a party of ten men of "C" Squadron, under Corporal Hurst, was sent down the Magadi Railway for detached duty on the border in the vicinity of the Nguruman Hills. This party was handled so successfully, with such dire results to the Germans who were unfortunate enough to fall foul of it, that Hurst was promoted first to Sergeant, and then to a commission.

Bowker's Horse returned after their arduous and short-rationed experiences to the comparative comfort of Kajiado, where they arrived at midday on September 13th. Alas for their hopes of a spell of high living (on bully beef) and deep drinking at Nazareth's bar! News had been received in Nairobi of an enemy advance across a far distant part of the border—along the shores of the Victoria Nyanza—and urgent orders arrived for the unfortunate two Squadrons to entrain immediately for Kisumu, and so by ship to Karungu on the shores of Lake Victoria. To add insult to injury, they were to leave their horses behind.

The task of entraining was no easy one. There was a certain liveliness in camp as the weary men were mustered for the journey, partially rested and impartially refreshed. At length the last trooper had been made to answer to the roll call, and at 10-30 on a dark and stormy night the first train, carrying "E" Squadron, steamed out of the station, to be followed an hour after midnight by a second train carrying "B" Squadron.

Passing soon after dawn through Nairobi, where the railway station staff came off second best in an encounter with a horde of hungry men anxious to break their fast, or anything else that came to hand, the trains reached Kisumu about midnight, and the force immediately embarked in the Lake steamer "Winifred". The ship arrived off Karungu Bay shortly after midday on September 15th.

The following account of their further adventures is another extract from *"The Army that Found Itself,"* as published in *East Africa.*

"We were crowded on the deck, waiting for the boats to be lowered, and arguing, in our simplicity, about the nationality of a red, white and black flag flying from a mound on shore, when two shots came from the shore and a bullet grazed the wrist of the man next to me.

"With us were a dozen Native Police Reservists, and their grizzled old sergeant jumped to it, yelling 'Come onne, boys, one t'ousand', and they commenced pumping volleys at the shore. On the edge of a manhole in the deck sat a native gentleman, who at the first volley dramatically threw up his hands and vanished down the manhole; he was found under a cabin bunk an hour after the scrap.

"There was a lull after the first two shots, which were probably the mistake of an excited askari. Then they turned upon us with rifle fire, machine guns, pom poms, and a six-pounder firing shrapnel. The E.A.M.R. —or Bowker's Horse Marines—were under fire at last.

"Mounted Infantry fighting their first engagement on board ship! But there we lay down in a packed mass on the upper deck and opened fire. There was little cover, and hatchways and bollards were much in demand. Some took advantage of a little pile of cases, until they discovered they contained shells, and moved hurriedly elsewhere.

"We had an ancient machine gun aboard, and it was rapidly in action under the hands of an ex-sergeant of marines. We also had a small Hotchkiss, and one of our lieutenants, ex-R.F.A., jumped to it and put in some fancy shooting. In fact, he scored a direct hit on the skipper of the German machine gun, completely silencing skipper and gun.

"Then from the reeds inshore ran a small steamer spitting pom-pom shells. A pom-pom ashore soon got our range, and scored a pretty hit with a shell that went through our awning and burst on the funnel, sending a shower of wood splinters over us.

"In spite of several shots like that, on the packed deck, nobody was hurt until one man got a shell splinter through the back of his helmet, through his spine pad and shirt, where it stopped and nestled snugly against his singlet. He was thrown into such convulsions, trying to get that hot splinter out, that several people were badly kicked.

"Another—the only casualty reported—had a neat centre parting cut in his scalp with a rifle bullet, but plenty of people had been grazed or had bullet holes through their clothing, and there were shell fragments and shrapnel bullets about the decks.

"We suffered mainly from fright. Over the water the pom-pom sounded like heavy stuff to our unaccustomed ears. We were firmly convinced that any shot on the water line would sink us, and that meant a 700 yards swim, plus crocodiles. When our own gun was first fired we nearly expired with shock, and turned to each other with 'where did that one go to' expressions on our faces.

"We most feared the steamer, which we were told was the captured British gunboat 'Kavirondo'. Actually, it was the 'Mwanza', which carried two guns (some say five) and looked wicked. The 'Winifred' ran backwards and forwards across the bay, and we chased from side to side as she went about, keeping up a brisk fire.

"Then some bright person reflected that the lower deck would afford better cover, so we dashed below, and re-opened fire from there. However, it did not look as if we had a hope of dislodging the enemy, and as the 'Winifred's' nice paint work was getting spoiled, we drew off. The skipper ran up a string of signal flags, and the enemy, thinking we were signalling to a force on shore, retired forthwith.

"Just after dark a red light was sighted astern.

" 'The "Kavirondo". Out all lights and stand to arms'.

"Matters were explained to us. The 'Kavirondo' could hole and sink us at close range. Our only chance was to grapple and board her, like Nelson's men of old.

" 'It was in Karungu Bay.

'Twas there the Squareheads lay'.

" 'No room to use rifles. Take knives and revolvers'.

"Men with hawsers were told off to leap aboard and tie the vessels together in deadly combat. The gleaming red eye came closer and we stopped our engines. The red eye stopped too, and a distorted voice hailed us through a megaphone.

" 'Who are you?'

"Silence.

" 'Put up your lights or we'll sink you.'

"Silence.

"Request repeated.

" 'For God's sake, put 'em up, somebody'.

"Somewhere below an engine churned, and slowly and dramatically our lights went half up, revealing the crouching figures between decks. Then it was our turn to call for their lights. We received no response, and little wonder, for their one light was up, and we were a passenger steamer ablaze with them. However, as they did not reply we lowered ours again, but were sharply ordered to raise them.

"Somebody recognised the voice of Garrett, the lawful skipper of the 'Kavirondo', but someone else said that Garrett might be talking with a pistol in his ribs, and it was well to take no risks. They lowered a boat, and just as it reached us some idiot let his rifle off by accident. The *flood of language that came from that boat dispelled all doubt. We heaved a sigh of relief, and somebody remarked 'They're British all right'.*

"So the 'Kavirondo' and 'Winifred' returned together".

In the meantime, at Kajiado, news was received that a German force, estimated to be a hundred strong, was occupying Longido Mountain, about fifteen miles over the border. Plans were immediately made for an attack on this force, and on September 16th the Headquarters of the Regiment, with "C" and "D" Squadrons and the Maxim Gun Section, marched from Kajiado to Bissil, continuing their march the next day to Kedongai, where "A" Squadron was already camped.

It proved that Kedongai was to be the home of the Regiment for many weeks. A further report by Lieut. F. O'B. Wilson—then attached to the Magadi Defence Force, but later in command of our Regimental Scouts—put a different complexion on the proposal to attack Longido, and the idea was reluctantly abandoned. Considering the kind of trouble we afterwards found at Longido, it is probable that the decision was wisely made.

While "A" Squadron remained with Headquarters at Kedongai, "C" Squadron moved about twelve miles away, to the stream at the western end of Orok Mountain; "D" Squadron was sent forward to Namanga, facing Longido.

This disposition of our force secured command of the principal waters, and was calculated to interfere with any enemy advance across the border. A picket was also posted at the Seki water-hole.

The Seki water-hole requires a line or two of description. It was only a small pool in an otherwise dry river-bed, somewhere in the bush between Bissil and Orok; but it gained a notoriety out of all proportion to its size or natural features. In the first place it was very difficult to find, as there were no landmarks anywhere in the neighbourhood, nor any well-marked tracks leading to it; hence parties sent out in relief of the picket were always getting themselves bushed. Then, when found, Seki was a most unpleasant place: it was crawling with lions, which made sentry duty a nightmare, as they prowled and growled around the tiny boma hungrily longing for a bit of horseflesh. It is quite certain that however hard the Seki water-hole may have been to find, no picket ever found it hard to leave. Later on Seki again became notorious, for it was while on patrol to that ill-omened spot that a patrol of ours was ambushed, as will be told in due course.

Though our proposed attack on Longido had been abandoned, it was not long before we found ourselves in collision with the enemy. "C" Squadron had marched from Kedongai to West Orok on September 23rd. There they tucked themselves out of sight in the thick bush on the mountain side, above the water.

They had not long to wait. Very early in the morning of the 25th, two Masai scouts, who had been posted up a tree immediately over the water, reported that a party of Germans had camped at the water, and had just moved off. The strength of the party could not be exactly estimated, but "C" Squadron immediately saddled up and started in pursuit, picking up the enemy spoor at daylight.

Travelling fast in open order, they followed the spoor, which led towards the Ngito Hills. They had covered several miles when, as they emerged from a patch of thick bush, they came in sight of a small group of native askaris cooking over a fire. Our men promptly started shooting, only to find that they had stirred up a veritable hornets' nest.

The Germans had been resting in the shelter of a donga; they were in far greater strength than had been anticipated, and at the sound of firing they swarmed out of the donga to the attack. "C" Squadron had only 26 men in the firing line, even though the barest minimum had been told off to look after the mounts. The enemy, as it was afterwards ascertained, were nearly 200 strong, including 35 whites, with two machine guns.

Advancing from the cover of the donga, and enveloping both our flanks, with their two machine guns in action, the Germans soon made things far too hot for "C" Squadron to stay any longer. The wonder is that our men got away at all, but get away they did, with four men wounded and eight missing, and retired to their camp at West Orok.

News of the engagement was received at Kedongai just before noon, two men, one of whom, Lance-Corporal L. F. Evans, had been wounded, having galloped back with a despatch from Capt. P. Chapman, the Squadron Commander. Two troops of "A" Squadron, under the command of Lieutenant G. W. Hodgkinson, were sent off at once in support of "C" Squadron, while word was sent out to "D" Squadron to attempt to intercept the enemy should he retire on Longido.

As a matter of fact, the enemy did retire, and very hastily. "A" Squadron was only in time to sight him in the late afternoon, making the best of his way back to Longido. The distance was too great, and it was too late in the day, to attempt an engagement. "D" Squadron got busy with enemy patrols, but failed to get in touch with the main body.

It demonstrates very clearly the comparative morale of the two armies at that stage of the war, that the Germans, although so superior numerically on this occasion, should have abandoned their project, whatever it may have been, and retired so precipitately. The scene of action, as visited early the following morning, disclosed eight graves, very hastily dug in the loose sand, and a dead native askari lying unburied; while all round in the donga were loads of food, and every other sort of impedimenta, thrown down and abandoned. The enemy losses are believed to have been about 36 killed and wounded, white and black.

Sad to relate, our eight missing men were all found dead. It is certain that some had been mercilessly bayonetted or shot while lying wounded. This, as far as recollection goes, was the only occasion on which the German askaris got out of hand when in action with the E.A.M.R. As a rule the German, black or white, fought us clean and fair.

Our casualties in the fight at Ngito Hills were as follows:—

KILLED:

Lce./Corpl.	A. C. Burridge.
Lce./Corpl.	Alan T. Impey.
Trooper	William Frew Somerville.
Trooper	Jack Leslie Elliot.
Trooper	Frederick E. Buller.
Trooper	Samuel Francis Edmonds.
Trooper	A. C. Forrester.

WOUNDED:

Lce./Corpl.	L. F. Evans
Trooper	C. C. de V. Wright.
Trooper	A. W. Adams.

In addition there were two men of the Magadi Defence Force attached to "C" Squadron on this occasion: one of these, J. D. Burgess, was killed; the other, J. C. Burgess was wounded.

Chapter Three
Longido

On September 28th "B" and "E" Squadrons rejoined the Regiment at Kedongai. There the E.A.M.R. remained during October, still keeping an outlying squadron at Namanga, and another at West Orok. The only incidents were occasional patrols after real or imaginary enemy parties.

Then the first harbingers of professional warfare began to appear in the form of Indian troops. It was by that time generally realized that any attempt to turn the enemy out of Longido must wait until sufficient additional troops had come forward to make up a column strong enough for this important undertaking. It was also becoming known that the attack must be made to fit in with the landing of the expeditionary force which had been detailed for the attack on Tanga.

It was on the 25th of October that we made our first acquaintance with Imperial Service troops when four companies of the Kapurthalas marched into Kedongai.

Four days later the E.A.M.R. moved to Namanga, where they were joined the following day by four companies of the 29th Punjabis, and the 27th Mountain Battery. With so many regular soldiers, so many Staff Officers with their red tabs, and particularly with the six good little guns of the Mountain Battery, we already imagined ourselves some considerable army.

A few days were spent in reconnoitring the enemy position, and in working out the plan of battle. It was at this time that Lieut. F. O'B. Wilson and his band of scouts did such good work, again and again making their way to the peaks of Longido Mountain, where they lay through the long days, concealed in the forest, spying out the German camp in the heart of the mountain, and endeavouring to estimate the enemy strength. Information was also brought in every day by our Masai scouts, who patrolled around the back of the mountain and brought in news of columns and convoys passing backwards and forwards.

Eventually the plan of attack was completed, and it was after this fashion. The main attack was to be made on the eastern ridge of Longido, from which it was known that the German camp could be commanded. It was the intention to occupy this ridge, and to get the guns into position there, before dawn. Another portion of the force was to feint at a frontal attack on the north, or near side of the mountain. Finally a mounted force was to ride round to the far side of the mountain, seize the water-hole which was reported to be there, and prevent the enemy from making good his retreat in that direction.

The strength of the enemy was not accurately known, but it was estimated to be about 600 fighting men.

The troops began to move on the afternoon of November 2nd.

Two squadrons of the E.A.M.R., "B" and "E" ("Bowker's Horse"), under Major Bingley, had been selected for the adventure on the far side of the mountain. One troop of "C" Squadron, under Lieut. Bailey, was detailed to act as advance guard to the main body. The remainder of the E.A.M.R., under Major Laverton, who had assumed command of the Regiment in place of Captain Sandbach, with a company of the Kapurthalas and a section of the Mountain Battery, composed the frontal attack.

The fate of these various columns must be related separately.

All went well at first with the main body. The column was skilfully led, in the dark of the night, to the top of the eastern ridge, and there before dawn the force was firmly established, without the enemy being aware of its advent. Unfortunately a thick mist hung over the ridge; in the mist a patrol blundered into a German picket, so giving the alarm. When the mist at length lifted, the fight began with attack and counter attack. Captain Sandbach, who had been detailed for staff work with the main body, was killed while leading an attack. Our advance never got much beyond the ridge first occupied. While the question of consolidating this position was being discussed, with the further important question of getting access to water, the enemy made a determined counter-attack, the result of which was the retirement of the whole of the main body from the mountain. And, as far as the capture of Longido Mountain was concerned, that was that.

The troops composing the frontal attack reached the foot of the mountain, where they came under heavy machine gun fire. Their job was only to act as a holding force: to have attempted any further attack from the position in which they found themselves would have been folly, and such an attack was never intended. Eventually, at nightfall, they withdrew to the kopje midway between Longido and Namanga.

The third attacking force, Bowker's Horse, operating on the far side of the mountain, had a more tragic experience, which must be recorded in more detail.

It must be explained, at the outset, that the instructions issued to this force, which was less than a hundred rifles strong, were to the effect that a surprise attack on the water-hole was likely to meet with little opposition, since it was believed that only a small party of the enemy would be found holding it. It was the spot at which the German wagon-road to Longido ended, where the

Germans unloaded their stores brought up by wagon convoy, for their porters to carry up into the hill. But, only in the event of our attack coinciding with the arrival of a convoy, or of a body of troops on the march, was it supposed likely that we should find the enemy in any considerable numbers. Subsequent events would suggest that one of these coincidences may have occurred.

The march that had to be made was a circuitous ride of many miles—twenty or so—over rough country, where wheeled transport was entirely impracticable. It was considered impossible that any followers on foot would be able to keep up with the mounted men, and so no stretchers or stretcher-bearers were allowed to be taken.

It was explained to the Medical Officer with the party, who was naturally anxious as to the care of any wounded, that the main body, having made good the position on top of the mountain, would thereafter be in direct contact with the mounted force on the far side, and stretcher-parties, if required, would be sent from the Field Ambulance attached to the main body, for the relief of the wounded.

It will be seen how woefully these arrangements miscarried. Our mounted party, from the time it set out from Namanga, never had any sort of communication with any other part of the attacking force. There was never a signal or any other message from the main body; while as for stretchers or stretcher-bearers, or in fact any form of assistance, this detail of the nicely-planned operation orders went completely west in the general collapse of the whole scheme.

The two squadrons had left camp at half-past three in the afternoon on the first stage of their long ride round the mountain. After halting until sunset in the shelter of the hills a few miles out from Namanga, the march was resumed under cover of darkness. It was as tedious and tiring as such night marches must always be There was no track; a way had to be found through the bush, far enough out to avoid observation by any chance enemy picket, short enough to get us to our destination before dawn.

Towards the end of the night a halt of an hour or so was made for rest—and contemplation of what the day might bring forth. The first light of dawn found the squadrons stealing along the slopes of the mountain, searching for the reported water-hole. By the time that it was realized that our Masai guides were at fault,and that we had overshot the mark, daylight had come, and a surprise attack was out of the question. It only remained to find the water with the least possible delay, and fight for it.

Wheeling in their tracks and galloping back through the bush, our lads soon caught sight of German askaris on the hill above, whereupon they galloped straight for the hill, dismounted and started light-heartedly banging away at the askaris.

A few shots in reply rang out from the hill above, and then, as our firing line pressed on towards the foot of the hill, firing broke out from the bush immediately in front.

The horses were hurried into a deep donga, which ran just behind the firing line, and our men, finding what cover they could amongst the trees, kept up a steady fire at the enemy concealed in the bush, not fifty yards away.

It was an impossible position. Our men were exposed not only to point-blank fire from the Germans holding the water-hole, but also to a deadly, deliberate sniping from the enemy posted on the hill above.

Again and again the troop on the left of the firing line, under Lieut. B. F. Webb, tried to get in a flanking fire, by climbing up amongst the rocks; but so fast as our lads clambered up the rocky slope the German askaris worked their way along above them.

To get possession of the water-hole was impossible, nor could the position have been held if gained. Our casualties were mounting up as the hours passed. At last, about ten o'clock in the morning, the order was given to retire. It was lucky that the retirement was effected in good order and without greater loss.

Unfortunately, two of our wounded, both apparently dying, had to be left behind in the donga, since there was no means of getting them away in their desperate condition. Two other desperately wounded men were carried out of action, but one of them died as he was being carried.

The Squadrons drew off into the plain, out of rifle range from the mountain, to count their losses, and tend the wounded. Of those missing, seven were known to have been killed; another, Corporal Furley, was reported probably killed, having been the last to stay behind, still fighting, when the retirement was made. There were also the two others who had been left behind, believed to be fatally wounded.

The wounded who had got away included Sergeant B. E. A. O'Meara with his wrist shattered, Trooper W. Nesfield shot through the head, and Trooper P. de V. Allen with a bullet through the ankle. Three others, including Lieut. B. F. Webb, were slightly wounded.

The little force then moved off a mile or two, to a kopje which offered a more secure position than the open plain, should the enemy attempt to worry us, and where there was some slight shelter from the scorching sun. Shade of a sort we might find, but water there was none. We had had no water since leaving Namanga the previous day, except that carried in our water-bottles long since emptied. Fighting under a tropical sun is thirsty work.

Despatch-riders had been sent round the mountain in the hope of getting a message through to the main body, but no news was forthcoming of the result of the battle elsewhere. Men could be seen silhouetted on the distant skyline of Longido, but whether our people or Germans could not be made out. The hope of victorious advance of our troops down the mountain-side, which had encouraged the morning's fighting, was now no longer entertained.

There was nothing for it but to return to Namanga. So, as soon as the dusk of evening afforded concealment, the Squadrons saddled up, and filed off into the bush.

If the previous night's march had been trying, this return march was infinitely worse. A stretcher had been improvized with blankets and rifles to carry Nesfield, who was wildly delirious and apparently in a hopeless state. The other wounded had perforce to ride, and to them that night must have been one long torment.

Nearing Namanga in the small hours of the morning, the weary party chanced across stragglers from the main body, making their way back through the bush, and for the first time heard of the general retirement from Longido.

It is no use blinking the fact that the attack on Longido was a dismal and depressing failure. Though that failure may not have directly affected the subsequent course of the campaign, it was, from its moral effect, most unfortunate. At the time, the fiasco at Longido was overshadowed by the simultaneous disaster which overwhelmed the British Expeditionary Force at Tanga. These two defeats completely turned the tables, so far as the morale of the British and German forces was concerned.

Before the battles of Tanga and Longido our troops were full of confidence. The series of encounters during the early days of the war in the Voi-Taveta area, where the K.A.R. and the Punjabis had so gallantly held their own against superior numbers, must have given the enemy good reason to respect our troops. Judging from our own little affair at Ngito, it might have almost been supposed that the Germans were "windy". Tanga and Longido changed all that: thereafter any windiness was all on the other side.

The failure at Longido was the more unfortunate in that the opening stages of the engagement were so successfully carried out, and promised so well. Neither our own men, nor the Germans (as they afterwards confessed) were able to understand why the promise was never fulfilled, and why the attack collapsed so completely, when the key to the situation had been gained.

At least the E.A.M.R. could not reproach themselves. Though no material gain could be set off against the loss of valuable lives, yet the Regiment had the satisfaction of knowing that it had acquitted itself well in its baptism of fire.

For gallantry in helping to carry a wounded comrade out of action, Troopers P. R. Heaton and G. le Blanc Smith were awarded the D.C.M.

Our total casualties at the battle of Longido were as follows:

KILLED:

Capt.	H. H. Sandbach.
Corpl.	H. M. Furley.
Tpr	E. W. Kay–Mouat.
Tpr	L. Tarlton.
Tpr	L. J. Moon.
Tpr	F. G Drummond.
Tpr	W. G. Bellasis.
Tpr	F. C. de Cerjat.
Tpr	W. A. Smith.
Tpr	T. H. Drake.

SEVERELY WOUNDED:

Lieut.	B. E. A. O'Meara.
Tpr	W. Nesfield.
Tpr	P. de V. Allen.

Tpr	F. Thompson.*

SLIGHTLY WOUNDED:

Lieut.	B. F. Webb.
Sergt.	D. C. Lunan.
Lce/Cpl.	A. I. R. Harries.
Tpr.	F. C. Shaw.
Tpr	P. J. Van der Merwe.

During the days that followed, our forces sat tight at Namanga, expecting attack. The defence of the flanks of the position was entrusted to the E.A.M.R. "D" Squadron was despatched once more to West Orok, while "B" Squadron was posted at Lone Hill, a kopje lying to the east of our lines of communication from Kedongai. The rest of the column was kept busy digging trenches and generally fortifying Namanga camp.

But the Germans had no thought of attacking, and were not even risking another engagement in their own stronghold. Ten days after our retirement from Longido, Masai scouts brought in the news that Longido had been evacuated. Patrols of the E.A.M.R. were sent to the north and to the south of the mountain for confirmation of this report, followed up by a party of fifty of the E.A.M.R. under the C.O., and by this party the mountain was occupied without further let or hindrance.

When the occupation of Longido had been completed, the disposition of the E.A.M.R. was such that Headquarters with "A" Squadron and the Maxim Gun Section was established at Longido West. "C" Squadron found a home in the rocks a few miles further along the mountain side. "B" and "E" Squadrons, after oscillating between Lone Hill and Namanga, were eventually allowed to settle down at Lone Hill.

---

* Thompson was one of the men left behind when "B" and "E" Squadrons retired. He was believed at the time to be fatally wounded, having been shot through the head. It was subsequently ascertained that he recovered from his wound, but died later of sickness while a prisoner with the Germans.

Since Longido West is a place of some importance in the history of the Regiment, it merits a few words of description. Situated at the foot of the Mountain, to the south-west of the Peak, the camp consisted of restricted areas of more or less level ground, intersected by rocky ridges, and covered with thick bush. To our front, the ground fell away in a gentle slope to the sparse forest and wide open spaces of the plain, which stretched without any prominent feature to the far distant foothills of Meru Mountain. Behind the camp, the ground rose steeply to the inaccessible precipices of Longido, from which there descended a permanent stream of good water. From these precipices there also descended, at sunset, a howling gale of wind as is so frequently the case on the western slopes of the mountains in East Africa.

Taking it all round, Longido West was a pleasant enough camp. The stream not only supplied plenty of water for men and horses, but also was dammed at one point to make a bathing pool, deep enough for diving, though careless divers found the rocky bottom uncommonly hard.

"Southern Water" was the official and somewhat euphemistic designation of the patch of rock, high up on the mountain side, where "C" Squadron was perched. It was more appropriately and picturesquely named "Rock Rabbit Run" by the cheery sportsmen who lived their care-free lives among the crags.

It was during the first few days after we had settled down at Longido that a patrol of "A" Squadron found the grave of seven of our dead, buried by the Germans on the spot where "B" and "E" Squadrons had fought their good fight. They lie there still, their last resting-place enclosed by an iron fence, secure against all disturbance by wild beasts, the rugged cliffs of Longido their noble monument. It is only by visiting the scene of that fight that one can realize the desperate odds under which it was fought, and the wonder is that from such a death trap our little force got clear away without much greater loss.

At the end of the year 1914 it was apparent that no general advance would be possible in the immediate future. There was certain to be a long spell of marking time, since the impossibility of an advance into German territory without further reinforcement from overseas was now obvious. Consequently a feeling of restlessness developed in the ranks of the E.A.M.R. Many who had joined up in the first excitement of war, with the hope of a speedy invasion of the enemy country, viewed with dismay the prospect of indefinite absence from their farms merely for the purpose of guarding the border.

To meet the situation, a scheme of "indefinite leave" was instituted. All those who could claim that their return to civil life was an urgent necessity (and, it is to be feared, one or two others) were given indefinite leave, on the understanding that they would only be recalled on the resumption of active operations.

Doubtless some such scheme was necessary. It was not only that many a man would have sacrificed all his chances of a future livelihood, by allowing his farm or business to remain indefinitely unattended during his absence at the front; there was the larger question of the present and future prosperity of the Colony, dependent to a great extent on European development. The continuance of farming activities was, in its way, as essential as the maintenance of the normal work of Government, the need of which was urged as the reason for retaining many of the civil officials in their usual duties. It was certainly as essential as the preservation of the commercial communities of the towns, where the slogan was "Business as usual".

The Regiment suffered a further loss about this time by the transfer of practically all the officers and men of "D" Squadron to the East African Transport Corps. At a time when the whole of our fighting forces were dependent on bullock transport, it was considered that the men of this Squadron could be more usefully employed in transport riding, in which they were particularly proficient.

A few elected to remain with the Regiment and were absorbed into other squadrons; among these was Lieut. Selby who joined "C" Squadron.

On January 16th, we said good-bye to "D" Squadron, as Capt. Arnoldi rode out of Longido West at the head of his men. At a later stage of the campaign Capt. Arnoldi was once more placed in command of a fighting unit, Belfield's Scouts, and met his death in action at Maktau, on the Voi–Taveta line.

At the time that "D" Squadron had ceased to exist, "F" Squadron, never strong in numbers, had also dropped out of the picture.

The disappearance of these two squadrons, together with the absence of so many men on indefinite leave, had the effect of sadly depleting the ranks of the E.A.M.R., and the result was to throw an inordinate amount of work on those who remained. In spite of the presence of overseas troops in the field, there was still great need for the local forces, and particularly for mounted men, invaluable and essential as these were for the continual patrolling of the border. It was no uncommon occurrence for an unfortunate trooper to be on picket duty all night, on patrol all day, finding time to groom his horse and attend to his own personal needs and comfort as best he could.

So great was the difficulty in finding men for all the routine duties that on one occasion, surely without a parallel in the history of any regiment, there paraded for a night picket a party of four consisting of the Commanding Officer, the Adjutant, the Medical Officer and the Veterinary Officer. The spectacle of the C.O. having his rifle and equipment inspected by the cold, critical eye of the Regimental Sergeant-Major was amusing enough, but it was a sad reflection on the attenuated state of the E.A.M.R. during those days of "indefinite leave".

However, in spite of all vicissitudes, the Regiment kept its end up. From Longido, patrols and larger forces again and again traversed the wide stretch of country between us and the German positions, seeking for the constantly reported parties of the enemy, which were always elusive and often entirely imaginary.

Christmas Day found all ranks at Longido standing to arms in the chill air of early dawn, it being supposed that the enemy would seize the opportunity to attack at a moment when it might be imagined that our gallant fellows would be scarcely recovered from an overnight overdose of ration rum. We subsequently learned from a captured German officer that, at the very same moment, our friends the enemy were engaged in the very same ceremonial, acting on the very same assumption.

The fact was that we were keyed up to a high pitch of expectancy, and our pickets were always on the *qui vive*; so much so that one wild and stormy night one of our sentries on a rocky ridge above the camp successfully put a bullet through the shoulder of his own corporal, to the great indignation of the latter, whose blast of profanity overpowered the howling of the gale, and conveyed to the surprised sentry that some slight mistake had occurred.

Such a state of expectancy—or in this case should we say trepidation—was responsible for the affair at Namanga camp, an affair which will go down in history as the "Battle of Namanga". It has been recorded in scurrilous verse. Briefly, the facts were that a picket posted by one of the Indian Imperial Service units then garrisoning Namanga reported one evening that they had been driven in by an enemy force advancing from the heights above the camp. All ranks stood to arms throughout the whole of the night, and all other posts in the Longido Area were warned by telephone of the imminent peril. In the morning the garrison of Namanga advanced to the attack of the mountain and fought a stirring battle with the loss of one Indian soldier wounded. The greatest difficulty was experienced in locating the enemy and the only tangible result was the capture of the horse-guard of "B" and "E" Squadrons by the 17th Cavalry, who were operating on the flank of the mountain. On the following day our scouts searched the mountain from end to end, but encountered nothing more hostile than a troop of baboons. Such was the Battle of Namanga!

Apart from small patrols, there were two operations of a larger order carried out during our occupation of Longido.

The first of these was a reconnaissance of the outlying German posts by two separate columns of mounted men and infantry, and a third party of Scouts. For the purpose of this reconnaissance, "B" and "E" Squadrons came forward from Lone Hill, to join the rest of the Regiment at Longido.

The combined force marched to Sheep's Hill during the daylight, as this part of the advance could be carried out under cover of the hills. At nightfall, the two columns set out, one bound for Nagasseni, the other Ngasserai. These were two isolated Kopjes believed to be held by the enemy.

The first column was misled by its native scouts, and did not reach its objective until dawn had broken. A surprise attack being out of the question and the enemy being seen in possession of the kopje, the column merely carried out a demonstration against the position and withdrew.

The second column reached its objective at two o'clock in the morning, and occupied a position above the enemy post. At daybreak our men opened fire on the Germans, who, according to reports brought in later by

Masai scouts, suffered several casualties. Unfortunately we had one man shot dead, Trooper J. F. E. Gale of "C" Squadron.

The third party, consisting of ten men of the E.A.M.R. and the Regimental Scouts, travelled from seventy to eighty miles on their reconnaissance, but the position which was to be reconnoitred was found to have been abandoned.

The other larger operation during this period was directed at the German post at Kampfontein. Our advance party of the Regimental Scouts and fifteen men of "A" and "C" Squadrons, after two night marches, reached the position before dawn, but fell foul of the enemy in the darkness. Shots were exchanged and two Germans killed. The intended surprise at dawn having failed, our party then withdrew. They were joined on their way home by the rest of "C" Squadron, which had been sent out to a kopje fifteen miles from Longido to cover the retirement.

There was one unhappy incident during the early months of 1915, which must be recorded. The horses and mules of "B" and "E" Squadrons were sent out every day from Lone Hill to graze on the slopes of Orok. On the day in question there was only one trooper on horse-guard, the other two men of the guard having been temporarily detained in camp, when three white men, in nondescript clothing, walked up to our horse-guard and without further ceremony made him their prisoner. They then proceeded to mount themselves on three of the horses and, with the unfortunate trooper tied to his own saddle, made off with the rest of the animals in the direction of Kilimanjaro.

The whole affair seems to have been carried out with the utmost coolness and impertinence, in the full light of day, at a spot close to the main road where our people were continually passing. It was this very fact that enabled the daring feat to be carried out. The uniforms of our troops in the field were so variegated and unorthodox, or even entirely absent, that the appearance of these khaki-clad brigands would have aroused no suspicion in the mind of the horse-guard, nor would anybody, who may have noticed them driving off the horses, have been led to suppose that anything was amiss.

It was only when the other two men of the guard were unable to find any trace of the animals or their comrade that the loss was discovered. Thereafter, patrols were despatched from every post to follow up the marauders and endeavour to intercept them, but they had got too long a start. The result was that the two Squadrons suffered the loss of practically all their animals, and, what was worse, the enemy were the richer by fifty-three good horses and mules.

The period of our occupation of Longido was marked by the appearance of an enemy less obvious than the German, but almost as menacing. This was enteric fever, which insidiously spread through the camps along the Longido line until it became almost an epidemic.

Enteric fever had not been greatly feared as a possible danger to our troops operating in the sparsely populated Masai country, where it could reasonably be supposed that the water supplies would be uncontaminated. The arrival of large numbers of Kavirondo porters, however, altered the situation. In spite of the most stringent regulations it was impossible to prevent the porters, addicted to insanitary habits, from polluting the streams. Although it was generally held that enteric fever was uncommon amongst East African natives, it is more than probable that these porters brought the disease and were primarily responsible for its spread. The swarming flies of the Masai country, the dust and the low state of the streams during the dry season just before the rains all helped in the evil work. Enteric fever was responsible for sending several of our men to hospital, and played havoc with the porters of the Carrier Corps.

Chapter Four
Bissil

The month of March brought the promise of the long rains. It had been decided by those in authority that the Longido line could not be held securely with the troops available, and a concentration on Bissil was ordered. Perhaps a daring attack by a strong enemy patrol on one of our convoys as far back as Kedongai, in which two Indian soldiers were killed, hastened the decision.

Longido West, which had been our headquarters for nearly five months, was evacuated on April 6th. The rains had already set in heavily and other units were finding great difficulty in getting their transport along the roads. But it was never the case for the E.A.M.R. to be defeated by transport difficulties. Our settlers knew too much about East African roads to be worried by a bad drift or a sea of mud and, after five nights on the road, the Regiment found itself encamped at Bissil—"B" and "E" Squadrons having been gathered in from Lone Hill en route.

It must be explained that, prior to the concentration at Bissil, the Regiment had been re-organized. Two squadrons had been dissolved and the remaining four were constituted as two wings, one consisting of "A" and "C" Squadrons commanded by Capt. Clifford Hill and the other of "B" and "E" Squadrons, commanded by Capt. Bingley. The whole Regiment remained under the command of Major H. S. Laverton.

Capt. Russell Bowker had been compelled to relinquish his command on account of age and ill-health, but the Squadrons which he had been instrumental in raising had so distinguished themselves in the field that they were accorded recognition as a self-contained unit, and so Bowker's Horse became a wing of the E.A.M.R.

It was during January, 1915, that this re-organization was announced, at a time when the people of Nairobi were being urged by the daily press and exhorted at mass meetings to realize that there was a war on, and to respond to the call to arms. Much as our lads in the field appreciated this effort to rouse the slackers that remained behind, they were amused to read that "real fighting men" were wanted; which seemed to suggest that those who had already borne the burden and heat of six months of active service could not be included in the category of real fighting men.

The following is the text of an announcement which was made at the time by the General Officer Commanding the Nairobi Area.

"I wish to make it widely known that more mounted men are of necessity to our military operations. The East African Mounted Rifles now number 170 of all ranks, and it is quite necessary that this number should be increased to 300, and more if possible.

"British East Africa's record in this War is of the best. Her Colonists have kept their country inviolate during the early days and without re-inforcements. She has supplied large numbers of her men not only to the fighting line, but also for the personnel of essential military departments such as Transport, Veterinary Services, Ordnance, Supplies etc. Nevertheless, it is quite certain that the small number of 130 additional men now called for, can be easily found amongst those who have, so far, contributed nothing of personal service to this World War, and could do so without any greater loss or discomfort to themselves than is being suffered now by their fellow countrymen in Europe, or has been suffered by their fellow colonists serving here.

"The terms of enlistment are the same as before, service is for the period of hostilities only. Indulgences include regular leave when military requirements permit, half rates on the Uganda Railway when on leave, wound pensions and gratuities as for the regular army.

"Recruits can enlist at any District Commissioner's Office or Police Post. They will be returned to their homes at Government expense at the expiration of their service.

"The East African Mounted Rifles are commanded by Major Laverton, late Major 3rd Hussars, and consists of two wings, the one commanded by Capt. A. E. Bingley and the other by Capt. Clifford Hill. Recruits on enlistment may select to which of the two wings they desire to be posted.

"I confidently look to all those in British East Africa who realize the desperate nature of the struggle in which the Empire is at present involved, to help and cooperate by all means in their power for the purpose of obtaining the extra number of mounted men so urgently required."

As the result of this appeal from military headquarters and the sudden wave of patriotism in Nairobi, the E.A.M.R. obtained a few recruits. At a later stage we received into our ranks certain conscripts, those East Africans who were compelled into the field by force of public opinion, after their sense of duty had been tried and found wanting, but who in spite of that were not unkindly welcomed in our ranks.

Bissil was to be the home of the Regiment for a period even longer than that which had been spent at Longido, for we remained there eight months. Our camp was placed near the crest of the low ridge which slopes upwards from the river on its southern side. It was an exposed, barren and uninteresting bit of ground, chosen on account of the good field of fire in all directions, but of this advantage we never had to avail ourselves.

During our months at Bissil we had as our neighbours the 17th Indian Cavalry and the 29th Punjabis, as well as, for a time, detachments of the 3rd K.A.R., the Rhodesian Regiment, and the 25th Royal Fusiliers. We also had a section of the Calcutta Battery, with its 15-pounder guns.

Life in Bissil camp was a monotonous affair of daily recurring routine duties, the tedium of which we attempted to relieve with football and other amusements. The monotony was also relieved for us by certain exciting incidents of real war, of which more anon.

The first onset of the rains being over there followed months of weather usual in that part of the country; cold, bleak days of cloudy skies, after the cheerless drizzling mist of the early morning had lifted. Patrols were regularly sent out before the dawn to make the circuit of Lemiboti, the commanding hill on our front, with the object of discovering any German force which might have occupied this position overnight. This patrol was aptly nicknamed the "bait patrol;" its blind groping through the dense mist of the dawn, with the continual anticipation of stumbling on top of a lurking enemy, was a most unpleasant business.

Other longer patrols afforded more variety. It fell to the lot of the E.A.M.R. to patrol the whole stretch of country along the border, from the Uganda Railway to Magadi Lake, as well as the "no man's land" around Longido. Still longer patrols penetrated deeper into the enemy's country—riding by night and lying "doggo" by day in any convenient patch of cover.

The time of the full moon was always made the occasion for one of these protracted patrols, the strength of the patrol being usually one officer and twenty men. A patrol of this size was too big to travel across country without risk of detection, while too weak to put up much of a fight against any considerable enemy force. When patrolling towards Longido, it was necessary, in order to cover the distance in the time available, to move along the main road and, for the same reason, it was impossible for an advance guard properly to make good the bush on either side of the road. Consequently it was a perilous adventure: it seemed certain that sooner or later one of these little parties would ride into a trap, since one imagined that the Germans must have discovered that it was our practice to patrol the road with the advent of every full moon.

However our luck held so far as the full moon patrols were concerned and the outstanding memory of them is the weariness of those long night hours in the saddle.

Perhaps one of the most nerve-racking of these patrolling experiences was when a patrol was sent to Ngare Nairobi, a German post far to the other side of Longido. The line of march took the patrol through a mile-deep belt of *sanseviera**. There was only the one road through with the wall of *sanseviera* close on either hand— a barrier of lance-like spikes terrifying enough to a man on foot and absolutely impenetrable for mounted men. The patrol passed through on foot, leading their horses in the bright light of the moon and expecting at every turn of the road to meet the fire of a concealed enemy. Fortunately for our patrol, on that night the enemy was not at home. When, later on, prepared machine gun positions and rifle-pits were discovered, cunningly concealed among the roots of the *sanseviera*, it was plain how deadly an ambush at that spot would have proved.

Less fortunate was a patrol of a sergeant and ten men which was sent one day from Bissil to visit Seki water-hole. About two miles from that spot they suddenly found themselves under fire from an invisible enemy. There was nothing for it but *sauve qui peut*. When the patrol rallied there was one man wounded, while four were missing.

The news was received at Bissil at five o'clock that evening. A stretcher party was despatched at once to

---

*A native plant much like ordinary cultivated sisal.

bring in the wounded man, but any attempt to find out the fate of the missing men was impracticable that night, as anyone who knows the thick bush of that trackless and featureless country around Seki water-hole will realize.

At four o'clock in the morning a party, thirty strong, rode out to the scene of the ambush. During the morning one of the missing men walked into camp. His mule had been shot under him, but he had managed to get clear away. Meanwhile the relief party, moving cautiously for fear of a further ambush, at length reached the scene of the affair.

There we found one of our men, Trooper John Dawson, lying dead, and two others severely wounded. One of them, Trooper L. Poyer, had been found by the Germans, who had attended to his wounds as well as they were able, and done all they could for him in the circumstances. The poor fellow had been shot through both legs. The Germans had offered to mount him on a mule, and carry him with them to their nearest camp, which was Longido, but such a ride was out of the question. So they left him under the shelter of a bush, having dressed his wounds and given him food and water—but they took away his rifle.

Our other wounded man, Trooper P. Ducrotoy, was lying not far off, where he had fallen when he and his mule were shot, so hidden in the long grass that the Germans had not found him.

What the feelings of those two men must have been through the interminable hours of that African night can only be imagined. The Seki water-hole, as has previously been mentioned, was notorious for the number of lions which haunted it. During that long night these two men, completely helpless, lay listening to the devil's chorus of growls and crunching of bones, as the lions devoured the dead mules within a few yards of where they were lying. Surely never was such a night of horror!

It is worth setting on record that when our men found Poyer lying there after his night in hell, his only remark, as he gratefully lit a cigarette, was, "I don't know when I have spent a worse night".

A grave was dug for our comrade who had passed beyond the reach of the pains and terrors of war, and his body was committed to the ground, secure as we could make it against the ravages of hyenas. Our two wounded were laid on stretchers, for the twenty-mile tramp back to Bissil: it was not until nine o'clock that night that the weary party at last reached home.

As regards the lighter side of Regimental life in Bissil, the chief distraction was football. The Association game flourished exceedingly, and inter-squadron matches were the occasion of vigorous effort and great enthusiasm. Then Rugger developed, to the mingled joy and suffering of those who battled with the ball on the iron-hard ground of our so-called "playing-field". After all, what was the loss of a few square inches of skin from knee, elbow or face, compared with the satisfaction of meeting one's sergeant, or even a fully commissioned officer, in deadly combat, and hurling him with joyful enthusiasm to the hard hard ground?

Then the Regimental Rugger team found itself, and challenged our friends of the Rhodesian Regiment, at that time stationed at Kajiado, who were no less keen on the game. We journeyed to Kajiado, to meet them on their own ground. The match was a good one, we broke a leg of one of their sergeants, and were right royally entertained that evening. What could man wish better?

The return match at Bissil was no less enjoyable, and the evening that followed, with an *al fresco* concert around a noble camp fire, was one to be remembered. Our score of games with the Rhodesians stood at one all; the concluding game of the rubber, which we agreed ought to be fought out at Tabora, was never played.

Our Rugger team even journeyed so far afield as Nairobi. This was an adventure fraught with grave danger, not on account of the prowess of the opponents we expected to meet on the football field, but of the many friends we were likely to meet in Nairobi bars. The team was given three days' leave. Fifteen good men and true accomplished the twenty-mile ride to Kajiado and the train journey to Nairobi without incident. They played their match against a Nairobi side, winning by twelve points to nil. Thereafter they regaled themselves exceedingly, with a net gain to the profit and loss account of the Norfolk Hotel. Finally, in spite of those who had foretold disaster, they returned to Bissil on the third day, all fit and ready to meet their engagements.

The entrainment of the team at Nairobi was a thing to be wondered at. The railway journey to Kajiado was a masterpiece of management. A certain sergeant, renowned in sport and war, confiscated all remaining whisky and took charge of a complete case of beer, from which he dispensed liberally but carefully and with a nice discrimination just so much beer as would ensure a suitable state of somnolence on arrival at Kajiado. So by beer and tact was riot stayed, and the destruction of Kajiado post prevented.

Concerts were a great feature of camp life. We had one performer who was a host in himself, and could carry on a one-man variety entertainment with a repertoire that could be adjusted to suit all tastes. There was one song which was never heard *in extenso* outside the circle of the initiated, but which, from a chance heard line referring to the amorous propensities of red headed curates, sounded distinctly promising. This talented soldier was the author of the regimental song which unfortunately can only be referred to by its title, "The Gentle Art", and cannot here be set out in full. Let it be said that this singer did not confine his singing to the care-free hours of evening. An outstanding memory is a dismal dawn of pouring rain at Bissil, with this merry songster crossing the parade ground through the driving storm, blithely carolling, "Hail, smiling morn, smiling morn"!

At Christmas time we arranged an extensive programme of sports consisting of a gymkhana, cricket match, and boxing competition. The gymkhana included every kind of mounted sport. At tent-pegging our champions held their own with the experts of the 17th Cavalry. Those less proficient in the finer arts of horsemanship got their money's worth out of wrestling on horseback and other forms of violence.

Chapter Five
The Two Affairs at Longido West

Two military operations in which the E.A.M.R. took a prominent part during the period of our stay at Bissil require detailed description.

At the end of July, 1915, a scheme was elaborated by which it was hoped to lure the Germans into an engagement, to their undoing. A mounted force was to travel rapidly and secretly to the distant mountain of Ngoro-ngoro, and drive off the large herd of cattle known to be on a European farm there. It was hoped that the Germans, on hearing of the raid, would send a strong force to Longido, with the object of intercepting our raiding party on its road home; but on arrival at Longido the Germans were to run into a trap consisting of a concealed force of the E.A.M.R. with their machine guns.

On July 26th the combined force of E.A.M.R. and 17th Cavalry set out for Longido West and moving by night arrived at our old camp. From there the raiding party consisting of two troops of the 17th Cavalry with the E.A.M.R. Scouts, continued in the direction of Ngoro-ngoro. With them went a large band of Masai warriors, who were to help in rounding up and driving off the cattle.

The third night's riding from Longido found the raiders approaching the German post of Ngaruka at the foot of Ngoro-ngoro mountain. By one of those mischances of war which can never be foreseen, our

Scouts rode into a Dutchman's waggon outspanned in the bush a mile or two from the German post. Shots were exchanged and thus the alarm was given. When dawn came our cavalry went forward at a gallop through the bush in the hope of rushing the post, but the few of the enemy holding it made good their escape, with the loss of two killed and others wounded, to a precipitous gorge in the mountain face. Here they were in so strong a position that there was little hope of dislodging them and no hope at all of capturing them.

It was obvious that, long before our party could scale the heights of Ngoro-ngoro and reach their objective, the main German force would have heard the news, and taken steps to attack the party as it was returning down the mountain. There was only one known way down, a narrow and precipitous path which was clearly impracticable in the face of any opposition.

So the idea of rounding up the cattle had to be abandoned. After destroying the enemy stores at Ngaruka the raiders retired on Longido. They were fortunate in having only one man wounded, and he able to ride his horse. There would have been no hope of carrying a wounded man by any other means than horseback across the seventy miles of wild country to Longido.

Meanwhile another accident had occurred at Longido but this time in our favour. In the early morning of August 2nd while our ambush party was lying snugly hidden in the bush above our old camp, a German patrol of white men and native askaris arrived, all unsuspecting, on the scene. Its advent was heralded by a single shot, fired by the Germans for some reason unknown, which effactually gave the alarm.

The Germans, still unsuspecting, began to off—saddle in full view of our men, when they were surprised by the appearance of four men of the 17th Cavalry then just returning from a night picket. They opened fire on the picket, wounding one man. Immediately the E.A.M.R. replied with a burst of machine gun and rifle fire. Within a few minutes the enemy waved a white flag, and Captain B. F. Webb promptly went down to take their surrender.

Those who surrendered were one officer, three other white men and two askaris. A party of the 17th Cavalry, which had been sent out to cut off stragglers, captured another white man running away, while a similar party of the E.A.M.R. caught eight horses and mules. Four other horses and mules had been killed.

It transpired that the strength of the patrol had been seven white men and four askaris, so that only four of them escaped and they lost all their animals. Two of the white men who escaped were seen by our maxim gun officer, and could have been fired on had the white flag not still been flying.

The report of the cavalry officer in command of the operations stated: "I was particularly impressed by the excellent work and markmanship of the E.A.M.R. Maxim Gun detachment. It was mainly owing to the moral effect of their well-directed fire that the enemy were unable to make any vigorous effort to escape".

Though the result of the whole scheme had not been on so large a scale as had been anticipated at its inception, yet it was a cheering experience for our lads to ride back to Bissil with their seven prisoners. The German officer accepted his fate as philosophically as could be expected, but blamed himself for the disaster which had overtaken his patrol. He need not have reproached himself, for the fate of that patrol was sealed from the moment it rode in under our machine gun position and no effort on his part could have extricated it.

The other major operation carried out from Bissil was on a much larger scale. After the capture of the German patrol, it was reported by our scouts that the Germans had occupied Longido West with a force about one hundred strong, presumably in the hope of turning the tables on us. Here seemed to offer a chance for a successful round-up, and plans were made for an attack on Longido West with a force strong enough to ensure the capture or complete destruction of its garrison.

On September 18th, 1915, two companies of the 3rd King's African Rifles preceded us towards Longido. The E.A.M.R. left Bissil on the evening of the next day accompanied by a squadron of the 17th Cavalry and the K.A.R. Mounted Infantry.

The whole column lay at West Orok on the 20th; there we heard from our scouts that Longido West was still actually held by a German force with at least one machine gun.

The plan of attack proposed that the E.A.M.R. and Mounted Infantry should occupy the ridges on the enemy's left flank. One company of the K.A.R. was to attack from the right flank. The other company was to clamber up the western spur of the Mountain, crawl through the forest and around the cliffs below the Peak, and then sweep down the ridge on top of the enemy. The 17th Cavalry would be in readiness, out on the plains below, to ride down the enemy if they attempted to bolt.

The preliminary arrangements were carried out exactly according to programme.

Just before dawn on September 21st the E.A.M.R. and M.I. were in position, lining the ridge to the south of our old camp, with their rifles aimed at the entirely unsuspecting enemy, who could be seen on a small kopje below us. We were awaiting the appearance of the K.A.R. from the forest immediately above the kopje. It was a question whether the K.A.R. could have succeeded in the extraordinarily difficult feat of making their way around those precipitous crags and through that dense forest during the night. They had succeeded. When the first askaris appeared among the rocks high up the mountain side it seemed certain that the Germans were caught like rats in a trap without hope of escape.

The appearance of the K.A.R. was the signal for firing to break out on all sides. Then occurred that which turned success into grievous failure. The first askaris, finding themselves under fire as they emerged from the forest, worked downwards to their right. They were unacquainted with the ground and did not realize that by working down the bed of the stream on their left they could have crept down under cover to within bayonet reach of the Germans. Those who came after followed the lead of those in front, until practically the whole company had drifted down to the enemy's right flank instead of being in a position to charge into his rear.

The position then was that the E.A.M.R. on the one flank, the two companies of the K.A.R. on the other, were firing on the kopje lying between them. An advance across the open ground from either flank directly on the kopje was too murderous an undertaking to be attempted. By the irony of fate the very defences which we ourselves had devised during our occupation of Longido West—the open clearings in the bush and the barbed wire entanglements—presented insuperable obstacles.

We remained for hours, E.A.M.R. and K.A.R., firing into the enemy from opposite ridges, bullets flying wide from either side falling among our own men on the opposite ridge. To add to the complexity of the situation, we found ourselves being fired on from above. At first it was imagined that the Germans had posted snipers up in the forest, but it is now certain that the bullets came from our own people. Doubtless some K.A.R. askaris, who may have dropped behind during the night-march over the mountain, on finding a battle in progress below them and being unable to distinguish friend from foe, directed their fire on the E.A.M.R. It was a mistake very easy to make since they would have observed the K.A.R. below them apparently firing directly at us.

By ten o'clock it was plain that we were not getting any forrader. We were suffering casualties from enemy bullets and from our own, and doing no good by holding on. Consequently, the Officer-in-Command of the E.A.M.R. asked to be allowed to withdraw with the K.A.R.M.I. from the ridge. Permission having been given, we withdrew without any difficulty, and regained our horses in the donga where we had left them before dawn. It was hoped that we should be able to join forces with the K.A.R., and combine in a general attack on one flank, without danger of further crossfire or misunderstanding. But, to our surprise, we learned that the 17th Cavalry had already started back for West Orok and that the action was to be broken off.

It was only when we were well on our way from the scene of the fight that we heard of the heavy casualties suffered by the K.A.R. As for the E.A.M.R. there were two men killed, one wounded and four missing, two of whom were known to have been wounded. Our casualties would have been lighter had not some of our men been trapped in the hollow between the German kopje and our firing line, having lost their way during our advance up the ridge in the darkness before the dawn.

So ended an action which failed so miserably that the memory of it is bitter. The column retired to West Orok mourning the loss of many good men knowing that the Germans had been left masters of the situation at a moment when they must have been in hopeless plight—their ammunition nearly exhausted and hemmed in on all sides.

On the following day the 17th Cavalry reconnoitred Longido West, and found it deserted. Two days after the fight a party of the E.A.M.R. searched the battle ground thoroughly and buried our dead.

The complete list of our casualties was:-
KILLED:

	Corpl.	A. W. Adams.
	Tpr. C.	Macmillan

WOUNDED:

	Tpr.	R. W. Anderson.

WOUNDED AND TAKEN PRISONER:

	Lce/Corpl.	C. K. Hilton.
	Tpr.	J. G. Dennis.

MISSING:

	Tpr.	J. L. Absolom.
	Tpr.	G. V. Jackson.

The K.A.R. had ten killed and thirty wounded. The enemy casualties were estimated at twelve killed and a number wounded.

Longido from the plain.

Patrol parading (with extra ammunition carried in bandolier on horse's neck).

Four of the Headquarters Mess
Capt, R. C. Wheeler (Vet. Officer), Capt. C. J. Wilson (Med. Officer),
Capt. C. M. Taylor (Adjt.), Lt.-Col. H. S. Laverton (Com. Officer).

E.A.M.R. Maxim gun.

After Longido: E.A.M.R. wounded.
(Standing) Lieut. B. E. A. O'Meara, L/Corpl. A.I.R. Harries.
(Sitting) P. de V. Allen, F. C. Shaw, P. F. Van der Merwe, W. Nesfield.

The E.A.M.R. Scouts.
(From left to right) S. Nielsen, E. G. Duirs, G. J. Pretorius, P.L. Swart,
G. C. Dovey (in front), W. H. Webber, L. Hawkins (in front), A. S. Williams (behind), C. J.
Brown, C.L. Saunders.

A patrol leaving camp

Chapter Six
The Big Advance

During the closing months of 1915 the regiment was kept busily employed in intensive field exercises while other preparations were made for the resumption of a general offensive. E.A.M.R. patrols were sent deep into German territory in the direction of Moshi and Arusha to glean the latest information of the enemy's dispositions.

On January 3rd, 1916, all leave was stopped—a sign of impending events.

By the middle of January our camp at Bissil was breaking up. On the 16th the Regiment paraded, complete with 1st and 2nd line transport, for inspection by the General Officer Commanding the 1st Division. The wagon transport took the road forthwith, and the Regiment rode out of Bissil at four o'clock in the afternoon of the next day.

Marching till just after midnight, we halted at the Sokota drift till dawn, then on by Kedongai and Signaller's Rest to Namanga. After a few hours rest there we took the road again at ten o'clock at night, bound for Longido West. Our column consisted of the E.A.M.R. and the South African Scouts, with first line transport.

As we neared Longido Mountain once again, we were cheered by the thought that this time there would be no turning back. Our column was strong enough not to worry about anything it might meet on the way, and our Scouts had already occupied Longido West and sent back word that there was no sign of the enemy.

So that for once, while moving along that moonlit road, there was no thought or fear of attack or ambush.

"E" Squadron was acting as advance guard. Word had just come up from the main body that the advance guard must push on more quickly, which meant that the files making good the bush on either side had to drop back into the road.

Suddenly, without the least warning the bush alongside the road blazed out in rapid rifle fire. The leading files melted away: the advance guard galloped back for cover, a stream of bullets following them. With the advance Squadron were some of its pack mules, which turned and bolted after the galloping horses, throwing the ranks into disorder. This avalanche of horses and mules crashed on top of the main body—unfortunately at that moment close up on the advance guard. For a few minutes all was confusion, men swearing, horses plunging, mules kicking; nobody knowing what had happened, or what would happen next.

By the time that things had been straightened out, and the E.A.M.R. were in readiness to advance on foot through the bush and clear up the situation, the order was received that the whole column was to retire on Namanga. We had four men missing, and one wounded—Trooper C. C. Chorley.

So much for our brave march on Longido! Our fighting force had been turned back by a chance encounter with a small enemy patrol (as we afterwards learned), which had had the luck to surprise us by a daring ambush and to shoot down our advance guard.

The spot was ever after known as "Scatter Corner".

We reached Namanga at dawn. An hour or so later a party of the E.A.M.R. rode back to "Scatter Corner", and found two of our missing men, Tpr. E. G. New and Tpr. R. R. de Donkele, lying dead on the road where they had fallen. We found the spot, only a yard or two from the edge of the road, where a few riflemen had lain. Judging from the piles of cartridge cases, they must have emptied their magazines as fast as they could shoot, and so given the impression of a much larger force.

The other missing men turned up at Namanga. One of them had crept away through the long grass after his horse had been shot and so made good his escape on foot; the other had galloped straight ahead down the road and then swung round through the bush.

That night the heavens descended on our devoted heads, as though in judgment, in an appalling deluge of rain which lasted till morning. With no other protection than a small groundsheet and a horse-blanket, conditions were, to put it mildly, distinctly uncomfortable. As much of our camping ground as was not a running river of water became a lake. One gallant Squadron Commander is said to have spent the night on his hands and knees, his groundsheet covering him from head to stern, and so slept peacefully while the torrent rushed around and underneath him: such is the advantage in adversity of being a hard case.

On January 20th our interrupted advance was resumed, and that afternoon we occupied our old camp at Longido West without further incident.

We remained at Longido until the beginning of March, our time fully occupied with patrols, road reconnaissance, escorts to transport convoys, and all the other multifarious duties of mounted men; while the camp filled up with troops, supplies and transport preparatory to the big advance.

On February 22nd we had a visit from General Smuts, who had then taken over command of the British Forces in East Africa. From a kopje above Longido West he viewed the country towards Moshi and Arusha, over which he had planned that our column should advance.

Our troops had been cheered by the news of large reinforcements arriving from South Africa, and we welcomed the advent of General Smuts as promising speedy victory; though our spirits were somewhat damped by the rumours of the serious reverse at Salaita, where the South African troops had made their first trial of strength against the enemy.

While waiting for the advance, the E.A.M.R. assisted in several attempts to surprise enemy outposts on our front, but without much success. On one such occasion the attempt was abandoned because of a terrific thunderstorm and torrential rain which brought our night march to a full stop. On other occasions the enemy were not where we expected to find them. Our friends the 17th Cavalry were more unfortunate. In a reconnaissance of Nagasseni, they were attacked by the enemy and lost two British officers killed and several men wounded.

After the visit of General Smuts we had not much longer to wait for the great event of the forward move.

It must here be explained that the general scheme of operations—intended to sweep the Germans out of British East Africa and drive them far back into their own territory consisted of a frontal attack by our troops massed on the Voi–Taveta line against the enemy's main body, while our Division, which had concentrated at Longido, marched round Kilimanjaro to take the enemy in the rear.

On March 4th the infantry battalions were trickling unobtrusively out of Longido, to re-assemble under cover of Sheep's Hill, whence the long march of the Division was to begin.

It was all-important that we should keep the enemy in the dark as to our proposed line of advance, and to this end every effort was made to indicate activity on the road we did not intend to take, that is to say the road to Kampfontein and Arusha.

Mules dragging branches of trees were driven along this road to raise clouds of dust and delude the enemy, watching Longido from far across the plain, into the belief that a large column was marching in that direction.

For the same reason, when the E.A.M.R. marched out of Longido West in the afternoon of March 5th, we took the Kampfontein road and followed it for several miles, only swinging to the left in the direction of Nagasseni after night had fallen.

The line of advance as proposed, and eventually followed, was by neither of the two existing roads. We know that the way via Kampfontein, to the west of Meru Mountain, was strongly defended. We had also learned from our scouts that the direct road from Longido to Moshi, round by the west flank of Kilimanjaro, had been rendered impassable for waggon transport by blowing up the bridges, and had been strongly fortified at every point of vantage.

The line chosen lay between these two roads, midway between Kilimanjaro and Meru Mountain. The choice of this route was due to the genius of one of our scouts, Sergt. (later Lieutenant) Pretorius. Relying on his memory of a journey made with an ox-wagon some years previously across this stretch of country, he boldly undertook to guide the whole column, with its guns and transport, along a trail which he believed he could find, and in the event did so with complete success.

At dawn of the 6th our mounted column was at the water two miles from Nagasseni, where, after posting pickets on the hills, we awaited the arrival of the infantry column, which had been travelling since the morning of the previous day from Sheep's Hill. On the arrival of the infantry the mounted troops advanced across the river on Nagasseni, to find this strong position unoccupied.

So far there was no sign of the enemy, no attempt made to oppose our advance. Far away out on our right flank, where a strong patrol of the E.A.M.R. had been lying up all day on a ridge overlooking another German post, a few Germans had been seen; but there was nothing to indicate that the enemy was as yet aware of the advancing column creeping on towards Moshi.

On March 7th the E.A.M.R. crossed the Nanyuki River to guard the right flank of the column moving forward to Nagasseni. The next day the whole force continued its march, with the mounted troops protecting the right flank, and camped that day at Geraragua on the lower slopes of Kilimanjaro where there were some European farms and houses. An advance guard which the E.A.M.R. had supplied for the infantry column had been fired on when nearing Geraragua, but after a few rounds from our side the enemy disappeared.

During March 9th the infantry remained at Geraragua, awaiting the arrival of the supply column. The mounted troops were sent off through the bush to the south, to look for a road and report on the water. We were fired on when about six miles out in the plain, one man of the 17th Cavalry being killed. We reconnoitred as far as a German farmhouse where we halted for a couple of hours, having found water, but no road; then we returned to Geraragua. Let it be noted that though that farmhouse was luxuriously furnished, with many valuable ornaments lying around asking to be picked up, not a single article was touched by our troops.

At noon on March 10th, the supply column having arrived at eight o'clock in the morning, the infantry column marched for Boma Ngombe. It was to be a long and tiring march, with many miles of waterless country ahead. In order that our animals could be watered as late as possible before setting out, all the mounted troops and the two batteries of South African Field Artillery were kept back until four o'clock in the afternoon. Then they followed in the wake of the Division, with a long line of transport waggons.

Four miles out from Geraragua, as we were nearing a ridge where open country gave place to thick bush, our advance guard was fired on, and immediately afterwards we found ourselves in action with a strong force of the enemy, who were directing a heavy fire on us from a spot over which the tail of our infantry column had only just passed.

"B" and "E" Squadrons, who were leading, extended into open order at the gallop, dismounted and opened up a rapid fire. "A" Squadron rode out on the right flank, the K.A.R.M.I. on the left flank, and the battle began in earnest.

Large numbers of the enemy could be seen moving about the ridge. Their bugle-calls rang out continuously, clearly heard above the rifle fire. The two batteries of guns had unlimbered in our rear, and to our great joy began to fire on the enemy position.

All ranks were full of cheer at the sound of the shells whirring overhead, and the sight of the shrapnel bursts along the ridge. It was an ideal opportunity, so rare in bush fighting, for artillery, and at that moment the enemy must have found the situation very disquieting.

But, alas, after a few rounds our guns remained silent: who can say why? There was a rumour afterwards that "someone" had told the gunners that they were shelling our own men: who knows? Whatever the reason a priceless opportunity was lost. The Germans afterwards confessed that they were astonished when our guns ceased firing; they said that their position on the ridge would have been untenable under continued shrapnel fire.

The enemy fire became more intense, and the Germans began to push forward from the ridge, opening up on us with machine guns from positions nearer and nearer to our firing line. From our left flank came the report that the enemy were working round in an outflanking movement and that in consequence the M.I. were falling back. Although our two centre squadrons held a good position in the centre of our line and a move might even have been made against the enemy's left, the order was given for a general retirement.

This was carried out successfully, the men mounting and galloping back, a troop at a time, to new positions in their rear, under cover of our maxims, which were posted on a convenient ant-hill in the centre of our line. Finally, the Maxim Gun Section mounted and galloped off, just as the enemy machine guns had started firing at unpleasantly close range.

Meanwhile the guns and transport were drawing off into the open plain away to our rear, until they came to a place which could be well defended. By this time dusk had fallen, and in the twilight the E.A.M.R. took up positions around the parked guns and transport waiting for attack.

But the enemy was not inclined to follow us in the dark any further into open country. We could still hear their bugles blowing along a wide front, but they molested us no more that night.

Our casualties in the E.A.M.R. included Trooper C.A. Sherwood killed, and Lance-Corporal L. H. le May, wounded and captured when the advance guard was surprised. Later in the action Lieut. R. C. Hill, commanding our Maxim Gun Section, as he galloped his guns out of action, was shot through the foot during the last intensive burst of fire from the enemy. There are various ways in which one may report oneself as a casualty, but this officer's method was certainly peculiar. He was galloping at the time side by side with the Medical Officer and suddenly made the surprising remark: "Can I see you some time when you are not busy?". Since the Medical Officer was at the moment particularly busy in getting out of the way of a most unpleasant number of bullets, this apparently fatuous question caused a certain amount of irritation and profanity, until it was followed by the intimation: "I think I've been hit". Sure enough, subsequent examination that evening by the inadequate light of a surreptitiously struck match revealed a bullet hole drilled clean through the ankle joint.

One other man, Trooper C. Scott, was missing, having fallen from his horse during the retirement. The following day, after Capt. Douglass and one or two with him had made heroic efforts under steady machine gun fire to ascertain his fate, he was discovered lying in hospital at Geraragua whither he had made his way on foot. Trooper Scott subsequently died from the injuries which he had received in his fall.

When morning came, it was found that the enemy were still holding the ridge. The Officer Commanding the mounted column decided not to attempt to force a way for the guns and transport until he was reinforced with infantry, and so we withdrew to Geraragua, with no further incident than long-range machine gun fire.

This engagement seemed to us a most mysterious affair. How could a strong force have interposed itself so suddenly, as though dropped from the clouds, between us and the tail of the infantry column? And why was the main body of the Division, only a mile or so the other side of the Germans, oblivious to the battle being fought immediately behind it? It seemed incredible that they had not heard the heavy firing, including gunfire, but the vagaries of sound in the African bush are incalculable. The Division was actually entirely ignorant of what had occurred, and was impatiently waiting the guns and transport while we were retiring to Geraragua.

What had happened would appear to be this. The Germans, deceived by our ruse when setting out from Longido, had concentrated to oppose us on the Kampfontein Road. Hearing too late that we had gone the other way, they moved across country in a hurried attempt to intercept us on the Moshi road. By the strangest of coincidences, their column crossed our line of advance at right angles exactly at the point where there was an interval of a mile or so between the main body and the mounted men. Sighting our force on the march, they fought us and beat us back, as has been described; but they were ignorant of the fact that the greater part of our column had already gone past. It was indeed lucky for the enemy that our main body was equally in the dark. If only the firing had been heard by the Division, if only our infantry had attacked him from the rear, his position would have been desperate.

Here is a strange commentary on the different angles from which a military operation may be viewed. On the one hand, our Division was blamed by British G.H.Q. for having delayed its advance to such an extent as to upset the general scheme of operations for bringing the Germans to bay: on the other hand, the German Commander responsible for opposing our advance was so chagrined at allowing our Division to slip through without bringing it to action that, so it is said, he committed suicide.

On March 12th, our mounted troops, with the guns and transport, resumed their march. They had been reinforced by about two hundred rifles from the garrison at Geraragua. This time we passed through the fateful belt of bush uneventfully, arrived at the spot only four miles on where the Division had been halted during the previous day, and then followed along the road to join up with the Division that evening at Sanja River.

On March 13th, Col. H. S. Laverton was appointed to the command of the mounted column and Major Clifford Hill took command of the E.A.M.R.

At this stage of the advance it became certain that our Division was to march on Moshi and not, as we had half suspected, on Kahe. The Division carried on towards Moshi, arriving there about the same time as the troops which had been fighting their way through by way of Taveta, on the other side of Kilimanjaro. The enemy had by that time retired on Kahe, there to make his next stand.

It is not easy to say what would have happened had our Division been directed on Kahe. In all probability we could have reached there before the main German force had been able to fall back after their stand at Latema-Reata Nek, and through Kahe was the only road by which von Lettow could withdraw his army in any form of order. But so important a point as Kahe must have been held in some strength. If we had found von Lettow's main force on top of us, while we were still fighting for a position commanding the road, the situation might have been desperate. Our Division was not so strong a fighting force as it appeared on paper; in fact its fighting strength was an unknown quantity. Unless we had been so fortunate as to have gained a defensive position of great natural strength, we might have been overwhelmed by von Lettow before the Taveta column could follow up.

However, it is idle to speculate on what might have happened. In the event von Lettow fell back on Kahe unopposed. Moshi had been evacuated before our Division reached there; and we were blamed for having failed to achieve the purpose with which we set out from Longido on our long march round Kilimanjaro.

While our Division was moving on Moshi, its mounted troops were pushed forward in a south easterly direction with orders to cut the Railway line at a certain point between Moshi and Kahe, on the night of March 14-15th.

Our own private opinion was that if the job were to be done at all it were well if it were done quickly. But orders were orders, and we imagined that it would not do to forestall events by carrying out the operation twenty-four hours earlier than the time fixed, as we could have done.

So on the night of the 13th we lay up in thick bush country, somewhere in the blue. The next day we carried on through the bush moving as undemonstratively as possible, crossing one or two rivers on our march. Of the events during that day one remembers only passing close to a herd of elephant and being attacked by bees while crossing a drift. It was highly diverting to watch man after man break into a mad gallop as he reached the danger zone. One gallant officer as yet unaware of the danger, unwisely thought the occasion opportune for a bathe. He was caught bending, and the bees had the best of it during his impromptu imitation of a centaur, as he galloped from the drift somewhat improperly dressed. When it came to the turn of the pack-mule which carried our two jars of ration rum, the moment was too pregnant with tragedy to be so amusing: but the mule was safely retrieved with the precious jars intact.

That afternoon the mounted column bivouacked, while "A" and "C" Squadrons of the E.A.M.R. set off to cut the line. The task was rendered no easier on account of the order that no explosive was to be used, nor had it been thought necessary to supply the demolition party with any tools. Perhaps we were thought capable of tearing up the rails with our teeth. However, volunteers with experience of derailing trains had been called for, and one or two of our troopers had most surprisingly professed to be expert at such work and had offered to carry out the job, armed with a large spanner which we had managed to cadge from another unit.

The two Squadrons set out on this cross-country ride, through trackless bush, led by Sergeant Hawkins of the Regimental Scouts.

It was a wonderful feat of guiding. The night shut down pitch dark and rainy, the flickering lightning flashes of distant storms only making its blackness more intense. As our column circled and twisted to find a way through the dense bush it seemed certain that we must become hopelessly lost. Even that exceptional scout Pretorius thought that we were wandering astray, and that we might find ourselves blundering in the direction of Moshi. But the compass carried by one of our men as a check, though its help was never needed by our guide, proved that in spite of all deviations our general direction was true and eventually, by what seemed uncanny intuition, Hawkins brought us to the Railway, at a point, as afterwards ascertained, almost exactly coinciding with the point ordained.

There, in the silence, darkness and rain, we halted for perhaps an hour, while our experts dislodged a rail: at every moment we expected the sudden flash and crack of rifles, but none came. Then, our work completed, we returned by the way that we had come, halting for two or three hours before the dawn to enable "A" Squadron, which had lost touch in the darkness, to rejoin; and so back to the camp in the bush whence the two Squadrons had set out.

Later we learned that the last German train had passed over that section of the line forty-eight hours previously, and that our only danger that night had been the chance of an encounter with a patrol of South African troops, which had been sent down the line from Moshi that very same night. Our party had received no intimation of the possibility of any but enemy troops being in that part of the country and a chance encounter with the South Africans would almost certainly have resulted in tragedy.

The fact that the expedition was fruitless should not detract from the merit of a difficult operation skilfully and successfully carried out.

On the morning of the return of the line-cutting party to our camp in the bush, the K.A.R.M.I. met a German patrol on the banks of the river about three miles from that camp, wounding and capturing one white man. The rest of the patrol jumped into the river and were probably drowned.

That afternoon the mounted troops rejoined the Division, at its camp on the banks of the Weru-Weru.

The next day, March 16th, we marched into Moshi. We had greatly hoped that our horses might have been spared from entering the belt of country around Moshi, which was notoriously infested with tsetse fly. But the move had been ordered, and from that day it was only a question of time before all our horses would be dead from fly disease. From then onwards it was increasingly difficult to keep up a sufficient supply of remounts for the Regiment.

Moshi, when the E.A.M.R. entered, was a scene of devastation. Every house had been rifled and gutted, everything destroyed. A roof over our heads was an unwonted luxury, but we were glad to get away from that ruined town the very next day, even at the risk of lying out all night in the rain; for by this time the rains had fairly broken and the nights were not all joy.

But the mere discomfort which the rains occasioned was nothing in comparison with the damage they did to the roads. After the middle of March, transport and guns found the going more and more difficult, until eventually all wheeled transport came to a standstill sunk to the axles in the mud.

Chapter Seven
Kahe and Arusha

The E.A.M.R. left Moshi on March 17th, with first and second line transport complete, and found a very pleasant camping ground in open hilly country, where we were far enough forward on the general line of advance to take an active part in anything doing, but not so far in advance as to be left in that state of splendid isolation which is apt to spoil one's sleep at night.

The Germans were now concentrated at Kahe, ready to oppose the next stage of the big push. On our side, all available troops were being brought forward to within striking distance.

On September 18th the E.A.M.R. were sent down into the bush country towards Kahe, with orders to see what they could find, but not to go too far. We followed a narrow and winding track through unpleasantly thick bush, and were not surprised when we were fired on; but it was only an outlying picket, which got away with the loss of one of its askaris. So we rode cautiously onwards, till we came to an open space; there we halted and posted pickets.

At sunset we received orders to return to camp, much to our relief, as the prospect of being cooped up with our horses all night in that narrow alley in the bush did not appeal to us at all.

At dawn the next day we repeated the motion, disappearing once more into the depths of the bush along that ominous track. On reaching the open space where we had halted the previous day, our advance guard came under fire, to which we replied, killing two askaris. Thereafter we sat tight, our advance squadron extended along the edge of the bush, firing on the enemy across the clearing and being fired on in return.

The E.A.M.R. had been told to hold this position so as to cover the flank of the 3rd South African Infantry Brigade, which was forcing its way towards Kahe somewhere in the bush on our left. So we lay all that day, face to face with the enemy, exchanging occasional shots; until, in the afternoon, down our road there came trailing a long line of Indian soldiers, the 129th Baluchis.

At their head walked a Brigadier. "They say you have reported that you are in touch with the enemy", said he, with a touch of scepticism in his voice. "That is so", replied our C.O. "And where might this enemy be?" said the Brigadier, still inclined to be supercilious. "Pass right on down the path", said the C.O., "and you will find out". With which the infantry passed on, and at the very moment that they emerged into the clearing the Germans opened up a heavy fire and advanced to the attack.

The leading Company of the Baluchis was just in time to extend at the double, and with a counter-blast of rifle fire drove the Germans back into the bush.

The infantry had arrived in the nick of time to save the situation: for our mounted men would have stood a very poor chance in that dense bush against the determined attack which the enemy was in the act of delivering. We were very glad to ride back along the trail, leaving further proceedings to the safe care of the foot soldiers who were swarming onwards past us in an interminable stream like safari ants.

On the following day we marched once again down the bush trail, to find the Infantry Brigade busily engaged in digging themselves in at the wide open clearing known as Store Camp. The E.A.M.R. rested on the bank of the river about a mile short of the Brigade.

During that day an unfortunate and tragic incident occurred. An enemy patrol sneaked up on the far side of the river, and surprised a watering party of our men. There was a sudden burst of firing, a general scatter of men and animals, and then silence. The roll was called, and nobody found missing from any of the squadrons.

Late in the evening it was discovered that Trooper N. M. Gibbs, the Colonel's orderly, had not been seen since the watering party had been surprised. It was full moon that night, and when the moon had risen, a small party went across the river to search for the missing man, but without success. It was not till the next day that his body was found under the bank of the river, where he had been shot down while bathing.

Instead of being left happily by ourselves in rear of the Brigade, the E.A.M.R. received orders at night fall to move forward to Store Camp.

Arrived there, we found the whole Brigade snugly packed into a strongly trenched and defended camp: packed so tight with troops and porters that there was no room for late arrivals like ourselves. The E.A.M.R. were allotted the open space immediately in rear of the camp, and there we picketed our horses, and lay down to sleep.

As we were composing ourselves for a quiet night two or three shots rang out. We cursed the snipers for disturbing us, and turned to sleep again, when the silence was shattered by an appalling outburst of fire. Snipers indeed! This was obviously an attack in force.

Our entrenched Brigade replied with every rifle and every machine gun that could be brought into action, and the pandemonium was shocking.

There we lay flat on our faces, entirely without cover, in the full light of the moon, deafened by the din, with the bullets cracking over our heads as thick as swarming bees. We vaguely wondered what would happen if the enemy attacked on the flank, a development which the

Brigade was trying to forestall by crashing off volleys from both sides of the camp. The staccato explosions of these volleys punctuated the continuous roar of machine guns with startling effect.

For hours the attack continued, while we lay inactive and almost past caring, half-dazed by the noise. At last, shortly before midnight, the uproar gradually died down, and we realized that the attack had failed.

This affair at Store Camp was one of the few night attacks the Germans ever attempted. It would seem that von Lettow, under-estimating the strength of the column advancing by that road, had determined to overwhelm it by a sudden onslaught, and for this purpose brought up all the companies he could muster, it is said to the number of thirteen, to carry the position with the bayonet.

The advancing Germans came under the fire of our advanced trench, and in fact never succeeded in forcing this, though they gallantly attacked again and again right up to the trench. Strangely enough and contrary to his usual procedure, the enemy attempted no flank attack; hence the immunity of the E.A.M.R. The ground in front of the Brigade sloped slightly downwards, and so the frontal fire of the enemy, directed at the trenches, passed just over our heads, and the hail of bullets, though disconcerting enough for us in our completely exposed position, actually could do us little harm. We could hardly believe, after it was all over, that the only casualties in the E.A.M.R. had been one or two horses hit.

The Germans left behind 19 dead, four wounded and two prisoners. How many dead and wounded they carried off, or how many more dead lay undiscovered in the long grass, is not known. It was always their practice to conceal their losses by carrying off their dead whenever possible, so it is probable that their losses at Store Camp were much heavier than would appear from the numbers reported.

The repulse of the night attack on Store Camp was rapidly followed by a general advance of all our forces on the main enemy position at and around Kahe. Any clear account of all the confused fighting that went on in that region of dense bush is impossible here; and since the E.A.M.R. took no further active part in these operations the story is unnecessary. We were kept in reserve, many men being utilized for despatch riding, escorts to guns, and other odd jobs.

The attack on the line of the Soko River on March 21st must however be mentioned, for here the E.A.M.R came under shell-fire for the first time. One of the 4-inch guns of the "Konigsberg", firing from Kahe, was dropping shells behind the firing line, where the E.A.M.R. lay in reserve. Though the shells did no damage we unluckily lost one of our number killed by a chance bullet, Trooper A. J. Mandy.

On the day after the battle on the Soko River, as the British forces were pressing forward after the retreating enemy to Kahe and beyond, the E.A.M.R. departed hurriedly from that sphere of operations, having received orders to make a forced march to Arusha, about seventy miles away.

We left Store Camp at 3-30 on the afternoon of March 22nd, drew rations for three days from a supply depot en route, and rode on towards Moshi. Our sole transport consisted of three pack-mules per squadron. We passed through Moshi an hour after midnight, and by 9-30 a.m. were at Boma Ngombe, after some trouble in crossing the rivers where bridges had been destroyed, and wandering about six miles out of the way owing to mistaking the road.

After four hours off-saddle in the middle of the day we continued on towards Arusha, until 10-30 p.m. By that time we had heard that the emergency at Arusha was not very serious. We learned that the danger that was supposed to be threatening that place was not from the Germans, but from the Masai, who had resented the manner in which they had been treated by certain of our troops (not East Africans) and in consequence were inclined to be truculent. Hence the alarm on the part of the garrison, who apparently imagined themselves about to be overwhelmed by thousands of Masai warriors, and hence the dash by the E.A.M.R. to their assistance.

We reached Arusha at midday on the 24th and found all well. Though our presence was really not needed we were glad we had come, and revelled in the joy of comfortable billets and plentiful food. After the privations of campaigning it seemed to us a land flowing with milk and honey.

We remained billeted in Arusha town for three or four days, and then moved out to a camp at Ngare ol Motonyi, a few miles out. It was a pleasant situation, near a good river, in fine open rolling country, and but for the heavy rains life would have been quite enjoyable.

The general advance into enemy territory had come to a standstill, on account of the impossibility of moving guns and transport wagons while the rains lasted. So the next month or so was spent in preparing for the next push, when the roads would be again tolerably passable.

Unfortunately for the E.A.M.R., this preparation involved calling on the Regiment for many of its officers, who were wanted for staff duties with the various Brigades. Other officers and men were taken away for subsidiary duties connected with supply and transport. An ominous sign was a request from G.H.Q. for a list of men suitable for commissions elsewhere. But what struck us as the most unkindest cut of all was to be compelled to surrender the majority of our horses, to make good deficiencies in South African units. This was a bitter pill to swallow, and it boded ill for the future of the Regiment to see most of our troopers dismounted.

On April 19th we received orders to proceed to Mbuyuni on the Voi-Taveta line; at the same time approval was given to the proposal to re-organize the E.A.M.R. into one single squadron.

We asked permission to march to Mbuyuni by the roundabout route via Longido, Kajiado, and the Uganda Railway, since the direct road from Arusha to Mbuyuni via Moshi was in an appalling condition of mud.

The E.A.M.R. left Ngare ol Motonyi on April 20th, at three o'clock in the afternoon. We had only enough horses for about one man in three to ride; the others plugged along on foot. Our baggage was carried in mule wagons.

We halted at midnight above Kampfontein. The next day we marched during the morning, rested during the afternoon and evening, on again during the night, and so across the plain, until we reached Longido West on the afternoon of the 22nd. After that we made good going, travelling for the last time along the old familiar road, through Namanga, Kedongai and Bissil, arriving at Kajiado at half past two in the afternoon of April 26th.

It was a notable feat to have covered the distance of somewhere about one hundred and twenty miles in exactly six days, at the height of the rains, taking our transport with us, and with more than half of our men dismounted. It was only the masterly manner in which our wagons were handled over the difficult parts of the road, and the dogged determination of all ranks to show what East Africans could do, that carried us through so well.

The Regiment entrained at Kajiado, and arrived at Mbuyuni on April 28th, 1916.

Chapter Eight
Down to a Single Squadron

On the arrival of the E.A.M.R. at Mbuyuni the process of dissolution began in earnest and the Regiment as such ceased to exist. Officers, non-commissioned officers and men were scattered in every direction.

It is impossible to relate in detail the fate of all those who left us; but perusal of the Nominal Roll at the end of this book will show how many of our number severed their connexion with the E.A.M.R. at this period of its history.

From such records as are available it appears that no less than thirty men were recommended for commissions in the K.A.R., as many again were recommended for commissions in other units, while double that number were discharged medically unfit, or transferred to less strenuous military duties elsewhere.

What was left of the Regiment was formed into a single squadron, under the command of Major Clifford Hill. Nominally this Squadron consisted of 125 officers and men, including maxim gun and signalling sections. Actually it never reached this figure, but took the field 105 strong.

There had been some discussion with the General Staff whether it would not have been better to disband the E.A.M.R. entirely at this stage. It was feared that the process of filching men for special jobs would still continue, and that the proposed squadron would be too severely handicapped, as the Regiment had been during its whole existence, by the constant draining away of its best men. Those in authority, however, decided that there was need of just such a body of mounted men, who could be relied on in any emergency; at the same time an assurance was given that no more men would be kidnapped. Though this promise was not strictly kept, and though the Squadron was soon to suffer still further and more serious loss from invaliding, yet an official statement was made at a later stage of the campaign to the effect that the retention of the E.A.M.R. had been completely justified by its subsequent achievements.

Mbuyuni, during that month of May, was a large military camp, where the greatest activity prevailed in view of the next general advance. During the rains our forces had sat tight, with Kahe as the furthest post in our occupation. With the cessation of the rains there was to be a push from Kahe, along the line of the Usambara Railway.

On May 19th the troops began to move forward from Mbuyuni, bound for Kahe and the unknown enemy country beyond. The next day the E.A.M.R. followed in their wake. We were only a small unit in a large army, but we felt sure that if and when anything was doing we should be well in it.

The general scheme of operations consisted of an advance of two separate columns, the one to move directly along the Usambara Railway, the other to march parallel to it down the Pangani River. It was to the first of these columns, under General Hannyngton, that our Squadron was attached.

The first job of work that offered was a desperate bit of bush cutting. The Squadron was ordered to safeguard the right flank of the column, and in order to carry out this duty had to cut its way, with pangas and anything else that came handy, through miles of dense bush. It was not exactly a cavalry manoeuvre, but we worried through somehow, and eventually rejoined the column on the line of the railway, and dropped into our appointed place as advance guard.

The succeeding days were each much like the other, full of apprehension but mostly devoid of incident. Mile after mile we worked our way along the railway—or what was left of it, for it had been systematically destroyed by the Germans ahead of us—and at every mile we expected to bump into trouble. Behind us plodded the infantry, four battalions of them, and somewhere behind were two batteries of guns; so we knew that any enemy force we might meet would be satisfactorily dealt with. But we also knew that the first blow would fall on the advance guard, and that whatever the final issue the E.A.M.R. would probably first take it in the neck.

So we pushed steadily on, past station after station, Lembeni, Same and the rest, only to find each one abandoned. Sometimes a few shots would be fired, but only by small pickets, which disappeared as soon as they had fired.

Apart from the anxiety incidental to advance guard work it was a pleasant enough safari. As we travelled daily onwards we had always on our left the splendid range of the Usambara Mountains, stretching away towards the sea. To our right lay the wide plains of the Pangani, where we looked for the far distant cloud of dust which marked the passage of the 2nd Division, crawling day by day down the line of the river.

There was exhilaration in realizing that we were part of a marching army whose object was the conquest and occupation of German East Africa: an army strong enough to overwhelm any opposition that the enemy might offer.

Of course our close association with a real army brought some of the minor worries of army regulations. For example, orders were issued for a "colour party" to be in readiness on arrival at each camp. This was a poser: what was a "colour party"? It then transpired that we were expected to have, as part of the essential paraphernalia of war, four little flags, to be posted at the four corners of the area of ground allotted to the Squadron at each successive camping place. So four little flags were hurriedly prepared, with blue letters on a white background; a piece of *amerikani* from the medical outfit provided the groundwork, an old blue puttee was soon cut up to form the letters.

The actual letters borne on our flags puzzled many a Staff Officer. On two of them were the letters "M.R.": that was easy, "Mounted Rifles." The other two, however, bore the letters "W.W.B.", and these had everybody guessing. The simplest explanation that could be offered was that the letters meant "We Want Beer". But certain fellows of the baser sort were known to declare that the symbols signified "We Won't Be" badgered and bullied by Brass Hats, Brigade Majors and other military what-nots.

The Pangani River after running parallel with, but at some distance from the Usambara Railway turns easterly until, about midway between Kahe and Tanga, the river and the railway run side by side. Hence our two columns, following their separate lines of march, converged on this point.

On May 31st the E.A.M.R. arrived at a German camp at a place called Bendela, whence the Germans had obviously only just retired, since their camp fires were still burning. There we rested, awaiting developments, knowing that the column creeping up behind us, and the 2nd Division coming down the Pangani, would find work awaiting them immediately ahead.

We were somewhat surprised when a certain South African General drove up in a motor car, and asked whether he was on the right road to find the 2nd Division. It was his turn to be surprised when he was told that he had only to keep straight on and he would assuredly find a very warm welcome, but not from our people. So he returned in the direction from which he had come, thankful for the timely hint.

Our belief that the enemy was not far distant was soon confirmed by the deep boom of a Konigsberg gun, somewhere to our front. As the gun continued to fire without any shells coming our way we realized that it must be the other column which was receiving its attention, and that the 2nd Division was in fact nearer to us than we had guessed.

In the fighting that occurred after our two columns had converged on the enemy the E.A.M.R. took no active part, so there is no need to attempt any description of it in these pages. It will be enough to say that the Germans were compelled to relinquish their last hold on the Usambara Railway, after a number of engagements, at the Pangani crossing, at Mombo, at Luchumo and elsewhere in the Handeni district. Abandoning the whole of this part of their Colony they withdrew their forces southwards, towards the Central Railway.

Although the Squadron had passed through this phase of the campaign without casualty from the enemy yet it suffered heavily from another cause during its march down the Usambara Railway and onwards across the Pangani. Night after night had been spent in malaria-infested camps, and the results appeared when men began to go sick by dozens at a time.

Scarcely a man in the Squadron escaped infection: at one camp fifty per cent. developed malaria simultaneously. Not every man who fell sick was left behind, for so long as a man could drag himself into the saddle he struggled on gamely. But as each day's march began there were some who had to be left to the tender mercies of the Field Ambulance, and so our Squadron grew smaller by degrees and pitifully less.

Depleted in numbers, but bearing up as well as could be expected under the depression of fever and short rations, the E.A.M.R. marched away southwards, as our columns followed close on the heels of the retreating enemy.

As we neared the Lukigura River it was reported that the Germans had taken up a strong defensive position commanding the river crossing. It was decided to carry out a wide turning movement, with the object of taking the enemy in rear, and our Squadron was selected to take part in the operation.

The march was to be made at night. At four o'clock in the afternoon of June 23rd a column consisting of the 25th Fusiliers, 2nd Kashmiris and the E.A.M.R. moved out of camp, committed to the hazardous adventure of making its way in the darkness of the night through trackless bush to seek out and attack the hidden enemy.

The E.A.M.R. formed an advance screen for the infantry. All through that night we marched. Morning found us still forcing our way onwards through a blind country of dense bush and grass which grew as high as our horses' heads. As the day wore on, and we groped our way stealthily forward with nothing in sight but a blank curtain of forest, it seemed impossible that we could achieve the object of our adventure. Of the enemy there was not a sign, not a sound.

Then, at last, a whispered message from the advance guard. The little Kashmiris push forward through the screen of mounted men, and are swallowed up in the jungle of grass. Suddenly, the crash and rattle of rifle fire: the enemy has been found.

Thereafter we became spectators of a spirited battle. The Kashmiris, who had marched so doggedly for so many hours of that wearisome night and morning, were held up below a ridge from which the Germans were pouring a steady stream of bullets from rifles and machine guns, backed up by a vicious little pom-pom, which spat shells with astonishing rapidity and disconcerting, if not very damaging, effect. Here was a chance for the 25th Fusiliers to make good their claim to the title of "Driscoll's Tigers"; and they were not slow in taking it. Charging straight for the enemy, carrying the Kashmiris with them in their rush, they drove the Germans headlong from the ridge, bayonetting the guns' crews and capturing the pom-pom and two machine guns.

It was quite a complete little victory. When we heard later that a battalion of Punjabis, advancing down the main road, had also got to grips and handled the enemy severely, we realized that it had indeed been a very successful day.

During that evening, as we lay in the shelter of the valley, the German naval gun began firing, with what object we could not imagine, as all the shells were bursting high overhead, harming no one. Possibly this display of fireworks was merely to demonstrate the absurdity of the idea that the Germans were running short of ammunition. Throughout the campaign we had been repeatedly encouraged by the official pronouncement that "the enemy's supplies of ammunition must be nearly at an end": and the end had always seemed a very long time in coming. As a matter of fact it was about the time of the Lukigura scrap that it began to leak out that another supply ship had got through our blockade of the coast, and that the enemy's supply of both ammunition and guns had been amply replenished.

Snipers at Longido West.

A group of officers.
Capt. Hon. A. Bailey, C. M. Taylor, Major Clifford Hill,
Lt.-Col. H. S. Laverton

Longido Central

Crossing a drift

Camp at Kedongai.

Our transport crossing Namanga River

The regimental soccer team.
(Back row) A. Milne, D. C. Lunan, V. W. Dunman.
(Middle row) J. W. Milligan, T. J. Noden, A. E. l. Craven.
(Front row) H. D. Tupper Carey, L. H. Le May, C. M. Taylor,
G. Simpson, F. K. Camping.

The regiment leaving Bissil for Longido.

Chapter Nine
Shell Camp and After

After the action of Lukigura the Squadron remained in camp for the best part of a fortnight. Then we followed up the rest of the Division to Msiha.

Msiha, or Makindu, or, as it was more commonly called, "Shell Camp" was a place which earned considerable notoriety.

It was at this point that the advance of our troops was stayed, while preparations were being made for an attack on a wide front against the next German position.

The Germans were reported to be preparing to make a determined stand at Turiani, where they had concentrated in strength. It was the intention of the General Staff to hold them there, until the South African mounted troops could be brought forward to carry out a wide turning movement. To get those mounted troops fit and ready for battle, and to bring them up to the front line, was a lengthy proceeding. As a result, our advance Division was kept sitting tight at Msiha for over a month.

Now the Germans had collected all available guns, including at least one of the Konigsberg 4-inch guns, at Turiani, and having plenty of ammunition they indulged in a systematic hate against Msiha, plumping shells into our camp at the rate of about fifty daily. For four solid weeks the E.A.M.R. lay in Shell Camp, with nothing to do but dig themselves deeper into the ground, hoping that no shells would fall among the horses, which had to be left standing defenceless in the open.

The camp lay amongst a series of ridges running down from the high hills on our right; every part was accessible to shell fire, though hidden from sight from the enemy. It was astonishing how little damage was done by the bombardment. Of narrow escapes there were many; but considering the total number of shells fired, after allowing for the large proportion of duds, the number of casualties was infinitesimal.

Only twice was the Squadron called on for duty outside the camp. The first occasion was a patrol to a village about seventeen miles distant, foraging for food. Only a small party of the enemy was encountered, which dispersed rapidly into the bush. On the second occasion we were called on to guard the road between Lukigura and Msiha to secure a certain distinguished visitor and his staff from any chance ambush.

The rest of the time was idled away, awaiting the sound of the first gun of the daily hate. There was always time, between the report of the gun and the arrival of the shell, to get to ground, unless one was too far from one's burrow. After going to ground it was only a question of whether a shell would make a direct hit on the dug-out, which actually never happened to any of us.

The behaviour of our native followers under shell fire was diverting. For instance, the cook of our Officers' Mess, a husky native of Uganda, full of a sense of his own importance and superiority, was duly impressed by the roar and bang of the first few shells. Then, observing no evil effects from such prodigious noise, he regained his composure, and walked about picking up hot fragments of shells with the greatest contempt. Until one day a 4-inch shell landed squarely on a cooking pot around which three of his pals were eating, leaving little of them worth collecting. Promptly our hero legged it for the hills, and was not seen again for the space of two days; after which hunger brought him sneaking back to the fold.

We managed to play two or three cricket matches, thanks to the regularity with which our friends kept to their daily programme of shelling. But it was difficult in Shell Camp to take even our pleasures otherwise than sadly. It was so humiliating, so intensely annoying, to be shelled day after day, week after week, by a fugitive enemy who ought at that stage of the campaign to have been almost at the end of his resources; while we, with the whole of the British Empire behind us, were powerless to retaliate.

The only offensive effort made from our side was from the air. The sight of our aeroplanes passing over on their way to hand out a bit of frightfulness to Turiani was some relief. But even the *ndeges* did not have it all their own way, for the Germans had improvized some sort of anti-aircraft gun. From Msiha we used to watch the shells from this gun bursting into little puffs of white smoke below our planes. It must be confessed that we were not too terribly apprehensive for the safety of our flying men. As we thought of their speedy return flight to a land of plenty somewhere near the Base, we agreed with "Old Bill" that "a little bit of shrapnel won't do them beggars any harm".

It was really the shortage of food, more than the shelling, which made Msiha a dreary camp. "Skoff" was very scarce in those days, as there was great difficulty in getting supplies so far forward. Of the necessities of life, flour and meat, there was barely enough to keep body and soul together: of luxuries there were none. Sugar was measured out to each man by the spoonful. The careful would make his ration last throughout the day by abstracting a few grains at a time from his hoard; the reckless would expend it all in one glorious cup of sweetened tea.

Sometimes we received unexpected additions to our larder. One of our officers used to prowl around the confines of the camp with a little .22 rifle, in search of game, feathered or furred. On the evening when he returned with a couple of fine fat cane-rats in the bag we sat down to a sumptuous dinner. One unfortunate fellow, whose stomach was not strong enough for roast rat, had to leave the table hurriedly, whereat his unsympathetic messmates rejoiced exceedingly and ate his share of the meal. It was perhaps too unkind when the remains of the rats were served up cold for breakfast next morning, for he of the squeamish stomach abandoned his breakfast also, and again the rest of the mess profited.

At long last the preparations for the turning movement against Turiani were completed. On August 5th we shook the dust of Shell Camp from our feet, and rode back to Lukigura, where we found the whole countryside alive with troops—horse, foot and guns.

During the next day the E.A.M.R. were kept busy helping to get transport forward over the road which the flanking column had to traverse, a road almost, but not quite, impossible for wheeled transport. Then the Squadron pushed on to join the infantry brigade which was making its way through the hills, on a line intermediate between the mounted troops on our right and another brigade working forward far out through the open country to our left.

The next days were typical of our East African warfare, for they reproduced the usual experiences of any general forward advance through bush country. There was the invariable speculation as to where we were, where the enemy might be, what we were supposed to be doing. Then, sounds of battle, near or far, mutter of rifle fire, thunder of guns—somebody in action somewhere, with what result who knows? We lay awake for hours one night listening to furious firing, only two or three miles away, but from a point to our front where, according to programme, there should have been none of our troops nor any enemy. Such is the wonderful uncertainty of bush fighting on a wide front.

Next day, August 10th, the E.A.M.R. assisted, though only as spectators, in a hard-fought battle. Our Squadron was held in reserve while the infantry attacked a strong force of the enemy, which was opposing the passage of our brigade through the hills. The casualties were heavy on both sides. As so often happened, night fell with the enemy still holding on, and in the morning we found the position abandoned.

The day following this engagement we marched down through the hills towards Turiani. A suspicious peace reigned over the whole country as we halted for the night within a mile or two of the position against which the great turning movement had been directed. What had happened? Had the German force been surprised and scattered by our mounted troops, or had the coup failed?

Alas, on the morrow, as we entered Turiani unopposed, we heard the news. Though the mounted column had succeeded in seizing a commanding position on the flank of the enemy, the Germans had withdrawn their whole force, with all their guns, safely across the river, and had made a clean get-away.

The Squadron lay at Turiani for a couple of days, and then put in two days patrolling in the direction of Kilossa. During the second day's patrol, eleven miles along a road which had been systematically obstructed with trenches and fallen trees, we heard away to our left the steady rattle of machine gun and rifle fire. The rest of the Division, pushing on from Turiani along the main road, had found the Germans holding the crossing on the Wami River. They fought the whole of that day. The Rhodesians suffered heavily in a gallant advance on the enemy's right flank. But once again a golden opportunity was let slip. The attack by our mounted troops on the enemy's other flank and rear was not pushed home, with the result that the German force again withdrew with all its guns and transport intact.

When the pursuit was resumed beyond the Wami River the E.A.M.R. once more shared the work of advance guard. With us were the K.A.R. Mounted Infantry, 17th Indian Cavalry, and some South African Horse, and on we all went towards Morogoro.

As we rode across the plain we saw behind us the smoke of a great grass fire, which seemed to be menacing the line of march of the Division. We learned later that the fire caught our transport column with disastrous results to some of the wagons and their unfortunate oxen.

On the second day's march we came to a hill on the top of which a small party of the enemy had been seen. After a long delay due to a misunderstanding of orders by our mixed and polyglot party, the E.A.M.R. were at last sent forward up the hill; but it was too late; by the time our lads could get to the top the Germans had slipped down the other side.

That night from the direction of Morogoro came the sound of continuous heavy explosions, and we wondered on the outcome of still another turning movement which was being attempted by the mounted troops. Once again we were to learn that the attempt had failed, and that the Germans, after blowing up everything which they could not shift, had evacuated Morogoro, and for the third time had got away with all their guns and transport.

Chapter Ten
The Last Phase

Our forces had now arrived at the Central Railway, which the Germans surrendered without further fighting. On past the railway our columns continued in pursuit.

The E.A.M.R., now reduced to a mere remnant of a squadron, were first sent off to Mikesse, which they occupied, capturing one German white. Thereafter they followed on along the line of advance taken by the 2nd East African Brigade.

On August 29th as the column of troops was plugging along the road towards the Ruvu River, the Germans started in to shell the road. Besides the naval guns they were firing a high-velocity gun, and the sudden and unheralded crack of its shells over our heads was particularly unpleasant. The mounted men sought what cover they could find for themselves and their animals, while the infantry proceeded to locate the enemy. Thereupon the usual confused battle developed, and as usual lasted till darkness called a truce.

That was a very uncomfortable night, for not only was there a considerable degree of uncertainty about the military situation, but it must needs rain in torrents all night long, and shelter there was none. Those foolish folk who feared a repetition of shelling more than rain, and had dug themselves shallow graves, were nearly drowned in them. Dawn broke on a very damp and disconsolate army; but the enemy had disappeared during the night. It was a marvel that they had been able to get any of their heavy guns away, considering the dreadful state of the road after the rain.

So forward once again, until Matombo was reached, when, after desultory fighting throughout the day and for once some artillery work on our side, the enemy once more retreated. At the crossing of the Ruvu River we had the satisfaction of finding one of the Konigsberg 4-inch guns, which the Germans had been compelled to abandon.

Thence on to Tulo, and so towards Dutumi, where the Brigade fought for three days before the enemy could be forced to quit. The E.A.M.R. were not called upon to take part in this engagement, but in the meantime had put in some useful work on patrol, chasing small enemy parties and capturing a few askaris.

By this time sickness, and demands for more of its officers and men for staff duties, had reduced the Squadron to such a small party that it could scarcely be counted any longer as a fighting unit. Its subsequent history must be related as briefly as possible, since it would be rather a flight of fancy to consider this period as part of the history of the Regiment.

Major Clifford Hill, with the few men left to him, was sent back from Dutumi to help in the work of getting supplies forward over the very difficult bit of country between the Central Railway and Tulo. There they worked from the middle of September until the first week in November.

Then this small party, this last remnant, was sent by train to Dar es Salaam, and thence by ship to Kilwa, to share in the adventures of the fighting around Kibata and along the Rufigi River. Months later we still hear of the E.A.M.R. in the Kilwa area, when it seems that at last with Major Clifford Hill only two men were left, Sergeant W. E. Powys and Trooper L. M. Joubert. These did excellent work around and behind the German positions in the neighbourhood of Rumbo Mission. All the others had been scattered on special work with various columns.

May, 1917, is the latest date to which the history of the East African Mounted Rifles can be carried. But the Regiment never died. It was never disbanded. Like an old soldier it simply faded away.

Chapter Eleven
Looking Back on it All

The preceding chapters have set out quite simply the sequence of events in which the E.A.M.R. played a part during the East African campaign. The question now arises, does this simple account provide a true description of the Regiment, and does it convey a proper impression of what its officers and men achieved?

As regards the truthfulness of the narrative it is to be hoped that there can be no question about that; but whether this true tale simply told can be supposed to contain a realistic description of the Regiment, that is quite another matter. The plain recital of events may recall to those who took part in them the vivid experiences of those early days of war; but for other readers there will be wanting those intimate details which alone can make the story live.

If the story as it has been told represents the Regiment as anything but very much alive, then it has been badly told. If it conveys the impression that the Regiment did not achieve so very much of military importance, then it has been told unfairly. Without a fuller background, without a more complete description of those early days in East Africa and of the difficulties which had to be faced in the early stages of the war, it is not easy to show in proper perspective what the E.A.M.R. really did accomplish.

It may be that in following the day to day fortunes of our little fighting force there has been afforded little indication of its important position in the military history of the years 1914 and 1915 in East Africa.

A difficulty in telling the tale effectively has been that the record is not one of military operations on the grand scale, of great battles and sensational victories, since with these we have not been concerned.

At the beginning, in August 1914, it is true that the E.A.M.R. stood in a position of supreme and vital importance. At that time the only other troops in British East Africa were the King's African Rifles, and most of these were well off the map, up the Juba River. One company that remained in Nairobi was hastily despatched down the railway, to ward off enemy attacks on the railway at those points where it ran nearest to the Border. So it was that Nairobi's only defence against a German advance over the Border at Longido was the E.A.M.R. Fortunately the Germans were unable or unwilling to attempt any such large-scale invasion. Their unwillingness may very well have been due to the presence in the field of a highly mobile force of mounted riflemen, whose morale was beyond question and whose proficiency with the rifle was likely to prove extraordinarily effective.

As soon as sufficient reinforcements from overseas had arrived in East Africa the situation was completely changed. Thereafter the business of the E.A.M.R. was not to be fighting pitched battles, nor to take the place of infantry in major engagements. If for no other reason, the Regiment was never numerically strong enough for such a purpose. At the first battle of Longido the Regiment numbered only 359, all ranks, and its numbers never again reached that figure. Throughout the greater part of 1915 the nominal strength was about two hundred. Even when the nominal strength at the end of 1915 was recorded as 297 the entry in the regimental diary referring to some particular operation reads: "The Regiment paraded 137 strong".

But if the E.A.M.R. were not called upon, and could not be called upon, to fight pitched battles, they were certainly called upon for their full share of every sort of patrol work. It was in such work that they were invaluable. The regimental diary mainly consists of innumerable records of patrols, large and small, sent off in every direction from every camp where the Regiment was ever stationed.

During 1914 and 1915 the E.A.M.R. were responsible for the patrolling of a very great tract of country. Our "country" extended from the Magadi Railway for about a hundred miles to the south, and from the Uganda Railway for about a hundred miles to the west; that is to say we had about ten thousand square miles to look after. Month after month that tract of country was traversed again and again by small bodies of the E.A.M.R. "on patrol".

The work which was done in this way was indispensable for the general scheme of operations, and it is difficult to see how it could have been done except by such a corps as the E.A.M.R. But it was wearying and exacting work, and the men who took their share of that work deserve full marks.

Comparisons are not only odious but often very misleading, so it would be foolish to compare the conditions of fighting in the East African campaign with conditions in the trenches in France. But, if we were spared many of the horrors, miseries and mutilations of modern trench warfare, there were anxieties, hardships and privations of our own special brands.

Riding on patrol through the African bush was always anxious work, whether by day or by night. One never knew what the next hidden donga or the next rocky ridge might disclose. It was the sustained tension of expectancy that was so tiring. Then, if it were a night patrol, as the long hours wore on towards dawn, mental strain was overcome by sheer physical weariness, which in its turn became a danger.

With the dawn the patrol would have found cover in some convenient spot. Horses would have been off saddled and hobbled, to find any grazing that there might be; but rest and refreshment for their riders was more problematical. Sentries would of course have been posted around the bivouac, but even for those not actually standing on sentry there was often an uneasy apprehension of possible sudden emergency to spoil the few hours of rest.

One of the anxieties peculiar to this type of campaigning was the thought—ever present even though actively suppressed—that disabling accident by bullet or otherwise might mean the miserable fate of being left helpless in the African bush, to die. Even the loss of one's mount might mean many weary and perilous hours of tramping back to safety through the trackless bush. So much of this adventuring was individual work. The members of a patrol might so easily get scattered, and so often it was a case of each man thinking and acting for himself.

If it was anxious work for the men of the patrol, how much more for the officer in command? He bore the responsibility for the safety and success of the party, with of course somewhere in the background of his consciousness the thought of his own safety as well.

The record stands to the lasting honour of the E.A.M.R. that they kept this roving watch over the wide no-man's land between the main British and German forces and kept their watch for a year and a half faithfully and well.

But patrolling was not the only work which called for fortitude and endurance. Every day in the life of a trooper of the E.A.M.R. meant hard living and hard work, with little rest and less comfort. The first consideration, involving a not inconsiderable amount of toil and trouble, was the care of the trooper's mount, whether horse or mule. In the case of a horse the work might be a labour of love, undertaken willingly; but grooming a fractious mule with its equally fractious companions in close neighbourhood was not all joy. In this crowded hour of the trooper's life there were undoubtedly more kicks than ha'pence.

One of the results of the constant knockabout turns with animals and their saddlery and other impedimenta was the frequency of veldt sores. These may seem one of the very minor horrors of war, but the discomfort of a crop of large and intractable sores on hands or legs or both has to be experienced to be appreciated. These veldt sores were difficult to treat and very slow in healing because from the nature of things they were always getting re-infected.

Treatment was not rendered any easier, and the appearance of the "patient" not made more attractive, when bandaging had to be done with ragged strips of *amerikani*—as was sometimes the case. It will not be believed that when application was made from Bissil for a supply of bandages the reply from Army Medical Headquarters was that neither bandages nor bandage material were "available for issue"! This during a period when a major engagement, with many casualties, might have occurred at any time. Fortunately *amerikani* was stocked by our faithful camp follower Nazareth.

When the long day in the life of a trooper was done there was often the night to be spent on picket. During the period when numbers were reduced by "indefinite leave" this happened to the unfortunate trooper more often than not. A night spent on picket is a poor preparation for another day of hard work. Sentry-keeping is a form of amusement which soon palls.

Standing on watch in the darkness of the African night—a darkness which is seldom complete darkness but rather a deceptive and mysterious gloom—peering at

116

half-seen shapes of rock and bush through the long minutes that seem like hours and the hour that seems like the whole night that is the time when the senses begin to play tricks, and fancy is apt to take charge. Those half seen shapes long and intently stared at seem to change to be coming nearer; and every familiar object of the daylight grows sinister and menacing in the gloom of the night.

Nor was it all imagination when the sentry seemed to see these shapes begin to move, and the bush to become alive, for our camps and pickets were always surrounded by every variety of big game. It happened that almost the whole of our field of operations was within the great Southern Game Reserve, and game was extremely plentiful. At Bissil one of our pickets a few miles from the main camp was posted over a water-hole, the nightly resort of all kinds of game. A moonlight night spent in watching the game coming to drink at that spot was a fascinating entertainment if it had not to be repeated too often.

Although we were in fact always in such close association with the wild life of Africa it would be unreasonable to make out that wild animals were responsible for a very serious addition to the dangers of the East African campaign, although they figured quite prominently at times.

Lions were a frequently recurring cause of alarm and a constant menace to our horses and mules. It was much later on in the campaign, after the E.A.M.R. had disappeared, that man-eaters were met with. The lions at Seki water-hole have been mentioned. At Longido West when the lions had been unusually troublesome one of our troopers killed three of them with three shots in the course of one night. When the E.A.M.R. marched to occupy Longido after the Germans had left, the advance guard was held up by seven lions.

A perpetual source of annoyance was the truculent rhino, which kept on popping up on all sorts of unexpected occasions. Once, when a party of troopers were bathing in the stream at Kedongai, a rhino appeared above the drift and charged down into the pool, immediately creating a very mixed bathing party. One unfortunate bather fled in his birthday suit down the only path leading from the drift, closely pursued by the rhino. On either side of the path were vicious thorn bushes; behind was the rhino, gaining rapidly. There was nothing for it but a flying leap into the thorn bush, and the unhappy man spent the next few days in extracting thorns out of every part of himself.

At the first battle of Longido an officer of the Mountain Battery had gone forward to see for himself the position of a German machine gun. He saw the machine gun, and the German machine gunner saw him at about the same moment, so he had not much time to waste in getting back. After a couple of hundred yards sprint through the bush he flung himself down behind a tree for shelter, and fell on top of a leopard! As it happened, the leopard was even more surprised and shocked than the soldier, and bolted without arguing the point. But our friend of the Mountain Battery was afterwards heard to declare that East Africa was "no place for pukka soldiering".

A milder form of nuisance was caused by giraffe, which so persistently brought down our field telegraph lines that reluctantly an order had to be issued for them to be shot when seen in the vicinity of the Kajiado Namanga road.

There is no record of buffalo having interfered with army operations. It was a sportsman from overseas who returned to camp one day with a story of having shot five buffalo—to be followed by an infuriated Dutchman looking for the murderer who had killed five of his best trek oxen.

In the earlier stages of the campaign, when the E.A.M.R. were holding the Border and lines of communication were not too extended, the question of supply and transport was not the major problem that it became later, when with ever-lengthening lines of communication it became the principal problem. Nevertheless our means of transport was not too assured and during the long rains became precarious.

It must be remembered that over the whole great tract of Africa in which the E.A.M.R. were operating there were at first no roads whatsoever. Behind us, as time went on, roads of a sort came into being, while drifts through the dongas and streams were made passable for wheeled traffic and larger streams such as Namanga River were even bridged. But at first there was no road at all behind us, and there was never anything resembling a road in front of us.

One result of the completely roadless state of the country was the difficulty in moving sick and wounded. It was difficult enough when there was some sort of track behind us over which wheeled transport could travel. Even from so comparatively accessible a camp as Namanga the wounded from the fight at Longido had to be carried back to Kajiado in rickshaws. When casualties occurred in engagements far in advance of our most advanced post then the difficulty was vastly greater.

The problem of providing for the transport of casualties from a mounted force operating in bush country impassable for wheeled vehicles remained unsolved throughout the campaign. It was one of the greatest anxieties of those responsible for caring for the wounded to know that a "stretcher case" would almost certainly have many agonising hours of most primitive and precarious transport before reaching the comparative comfort of a stationary dressing station or hospital.

It was later in the campaign, towards the end of the brief existence of the E.A.M.R., that transport became so difficult as to bring hunger very prominently into the picture. Thereafter hunger became the East African campaigner's constant companion.

It was in the later stages too that the advance carried the Regiment into country so unhealthy for man and beast that malaria became practically universal and all the animals were fly-stricken. There came the toughest test of stamina and endurance when it was a matter of carrying on week after week through endless miles of marching under the debilitating and deadly depression of continually recurring attacks of malaria. When, towards the very end, there was a change of medical officers, the incoming medico promptly pronounced the remnant of the Regiment to be only fit for wholesale invaliding, a pronouncement which was characteristically disregarded.

Finally, looking back on it all and trying to judge impartially what the E.A.M.R. accomplished, there is one point which must be emphasized again. As was explained in the introduction to this story, the Regiment suffered during the whole of its existence from the continual draining away of its officers and men to other units. This constant process of depletion was a terrible handicap. It was impossible for the Regiment really to "find itself" as a properly organised and fully developed fighting unit while it suffered from such a disadvantage.

This point is not put forward here as an excuse for anything the Regiment failed to do, since it never failed in what it had to do. Rather the point is this, that whatever the E.A.M.R. lost in this process of disintegration other units gained. Not the least of the services which the E.A.M.R. rendered to East Africa was this constant supply of so many men for essential services elsewhere. It was a most admirable Officers' Training Corps, and though the training was hard the results were excellent. In trying to sum up what the Regiment accomplished it would be only fair to take into account the subsequent achievements of those who passed through its ranks to other military duties.

Honour is due to those who served with the Regiment to the end. Honour no less is due to those who were called away for service elsewhere. But the highest honour is theirs who died fighting for King and Country, and it is by virtue of their supreme sacrifice that the honour of the Regiment stands and the memory of the East African Mounted Rifles will endure.

Appendix A.

The Scouts

(By Captain F. O'B. Wilson, C.M.G., D.S.O.)

We came into being at the outbreak of War as the Magadi Defence Corps—a small and mixed party gathered together haphazard.

Of the original eight, one was a railway guard, one a chemist, one an accountant, another a builder, with farmers and big game hunters making up the number. The force was mounted on mules and armed with every kind of rifle except the Service .303.

The Patrol was sent out from Kajiado to try and find a possible road to the German Border. The country through which the road was to be found was reported to be a waterless and impassable desert from Bissil onwards.

Dangers from Germans, tsetse fly and the desert which loomed large on the first patrol soon dwindled, but camping and moving at night provided all the spice and excitement that was wanted. The country swarmed with game of every description; lion, rhino and elephant abounded. Large fires had to be kept up all night to keep the lions from attacking the mules and stampeding them. The dangers from wild animals were more guarded against than possible surprise from the enemy.

The trip soon developed into little more than a most interesting safari in unknown country. A sixty mile walk from Manga River to Kajiado caused by the stampede of the mules by an inquisitive hippo helped to keep the patrol in hard condition.

Having found the road the next job was to reconnoitre Longido, where the Germans were believed to have a camp.

This was generally done by setting out at dusk from Manga and riding through the bush to some secluded spot at the base of the mountain. An ascent on foot in the darkness would then be made to some spot commanding the Hun camps, and a pleasant and restful day could then be spent in the forest watching our adversaries at their daily routine, while the patrol endeavoured to get some idea of their strength and disposition.

This peaceful method of making war continued until the evacuation of Longido by the Germans which followed soon after the attack on Longido on November 4th, 1914.

When the enemy withdrew from Longido the *raison d'être* of the Magadi Defence Corps lapsed and they then became in name what they had been all the time, the E.A.M.R. Scouts.

In view of the bigger distances which would in future have to be covered they were now mounted on the best and fastest horses that could be found in Kenya. The best of the mules were reduced to the status of pack animals. From that time until April, 1916 the Scouts were a body of men varying in numbers from eight to twelve, really well mounted and provided with pack mule transport. The mules showed their appreciation at having their loads reduced from 200 lbs. of rider and equipment to 100 Lbs. Each mule adopted one of the horses as his particular friend and in times of stress they would close on to their horses and refuse to be separated, no matter how fast the horses might gallop. On occasions of rapid retreat the pace sometimes became a racing speed yet the little mules would keep right up each with his own horse.

After the evacuation of Longido the Scouts' work consisted of reconnoitring the enemy positions on the slopes of Kilimanjaro and Meru and on occasion exploring the country west of Longido towards Ketumbeni and up to the slopes of Ngorongoro. With such a sparsely populated area of country in which to operate, the dangers to a small rapidly moving patrol consisted more in being deprived of water than of being caught by the enemy. The troop sometimes worked as far as thirty to forty miles behind the German lines, travelling by night and lying up by day. On one occasion when circumstances made it necessary to cover a hundred miles in twenty-four hours before water could be reached the value of having good mounts was well demonstrated.

On the whole, encounters with the enemy were few, but a knowledge of the country was gained which became useful when the advance of 1916 took place.

At the expiration of this advance the service of the Scouts was no longer needed and they dispersed.

On the road to Longido West.

Scouting.

Patrol watering at a drift.

A bivouac in the bush.

Mounts turned out to graze.

The first camouflaged pony.

Horse lines, showing camouflaged ponies.

Appendix B
Some Memories of the Last Phases

(By Major Clifford Hill, D.S.O.)

The first phase of the East African Campaign had ended. Moshi and Arusha were in the hands of the British Forces. The country had received reinforcements and several thousands of mounted troops had arrived.

What of the E.A.M.R.? Conjecture was rife in the ranks, there was a feeling that the Regiment would no longer exist as a unit. The many newly-raised battalions of the K.A.R. were crying for officers, so were Supplies, Scouts, the Intelligence Department and the rest. Even the recently arrived regiments from South Africa, both mounted and foot, must have someone who could converse with the natives and who would know something of local conditions. For the Military Labour Bureau such men were indispensable.

It therefore came somewhat as a surprise to all ranks when it was made known that the Regiment would carry on, much depleted in numbers but with machine guns and followers complete.

One or two of the staff went straight to Mbuyuni and were soon in the throes of the reorganisation. Most of this work devolved upon the devoted Quartermaster, Capt. J. W. Milligan, and the Adjutant, Captain C. M. Taylor, both of whom had been with the Regiment since its very beginning and both of whom, alas, were taking up other important posts in the Service and would not continue with the reorganised unit. The Commanding Officer, Colonel H. S. Laverton was called away to take over an important post elsewhere, and the command devolved upon myself.

It was while these changes were taking place, after the decision to retain the E.A.M.R. had been reached, that the General Officer commanding the First East African Division said: "It gives me great satisfaction to know that I have at hand a body of tried men whose special qualifications I know and upon whom I can count to carry out certain operations which no other unit can possibly perform, operations which may and will call for special knowledge of country, language and dealings with the natives, in addition to the usual routine work of scouting and fighting. I consider the retention of the E.A.M.R. as a unit essential".

Two months after leaving Mbuyuni the E.A.M.R. had arrived at Msiha, or "Shell Camp" where for several weeks the Camp was subject to quite severe shelling, for East Africa. On one occasion as many as fifty shells fell within an hour.

At the beginning of August the enemy guns were still very busy but there were signs that the long wait was coming to an end and on August 6th British columns were on the move against the enemy positions. Transport moved out from Lukigura on the 7th, the escort consisting of the 25th Royal Fusiliers under Colonel Driscoll and the E.A.M.R. One troop of the E.A.M.R. formed the advance guard and another was rearguard to the column.

The long wait before the advance had been disastrous to the transport animals. All day the weary fly stricken creatures were attempting in vain to drag the loads up the hills; by evening the rearguard was a short five miles from the start, and the country there was waterless. All the E.A.M.R. animals were sent back after dark to drink and return; this was a lucky move as orders came for the

E.A.M.R. to move to advance Headquarters at day break and report to the general there.

At 5 a.m. the Squadron was on the move and it was apparent to us as we passed lines of wagons that the weary animals had shot their bolt and would not survive more than another day or so, especially as many of them had not had a drink since the evening of the 6th before leaving Lukigura.

At Headquarters was the Commander-in-Chief General Smuts, and with him the Divisional General. "What of the transport?" asked the C.-in-C. as the Squadron rode up. "I am convinced that because of tsetse fly and lack of water the transport will not get through this way", was my reply. "That settles it; I thought so", remarked the C.-in-C. turning to General Hoskins, "Everything must return and go by the other route. Keep Divisional and "B" Column rations and do what you can to get them through to Hannyngton."

General Hoskins explained the position. "B" Column under General Hannyngton was already in contact with the enemy and expected to be up against the main position that day. Two days rations to last three days had gone with the column and it was essential to replenish these by the next day. A plan was immediately evolved: all our men's blankets and kit would go on the return carts to be picked up later on during the advance, the men would push on with stripped saddles, walking, while all the mules and horses and a number of followers would be laden with the necessary food.

It was hardly expected that any enemy would be encountered before joining up with "B" Column. That evening the Loyal North Lancs Machine gunners arrived; their animals had had no water for two days and were terrible thirsty, but received a little that night. Next evening after dark all supplies had reached "B" Column, and a weary band of E.A.M.R. were attending to their mounts, which had been led along all day laden with rations, when the General himself came along to the lines and shattered all hopes of a restful morning by informing us that he had plans for using the E.A.M.R. in connection with next day's fighting and this would entail leaving camp next morning in the dark to take up a position in the rear of the German advanced position. This position was to be attacked at daylight and the enemy holding it driven back on their main force, entrenched a few miles further on. The E.A.M.R. assisted by the K.A.R. Mounted Infantry would attack the retiring German force between the two positions. A good I.D. man and a local native would act as guides to the place selected for the ambush.

Before daybreak next morning the small mounted force, about fifty rifles in all, was on the move through the bush. After going for about an hour and a half I sent for the native guide and asked him why it was taking so much time to get to the spot. It then appeared that the native was making for the main German position and not for any intermediate spot at all; I promptly took matters into my own hands, changed direction to the right, and in a very short time halted the force on a slight heavily wooded rise overlooking the track near a mtama field, with a fair sized stream on the left. In the mean time I went down with an orderly to examine the track.

A few scattered shots were being fired a couple of miles up the path towards Hannyngton's advance, but it was apparent from the tracks on the path that the bulk of the enemy had already fallen back. At that moment round the bend of the road not a dozen yards from us came a German patrol, but before they had time to raise their rifles a burst of fire from the ridge sent both friend and enemy head first into the dense bush at the side of the road with apparently no one hit on either side.

Contact was made with the advancing infantry after about four hours, and the infantry advance cautiously pushed forward to the stream and some distance up the further slope when the General and his staff came along. They stopped and had a chat with the officers of the mounted troop, and the General suggested that the animals might go down to the stream for water.

With a glance at the ridge on the far side I expressed the opinion that the horses might be allowed to cool off a little longer before venturing down. A fierce crackle of rifles from the ridge a few minutes later confirmed the wisdom of that opinion; once again, as at Kahe, the infantry had arrived at an opportune moment.

That afternoon and all the next day the fighting was severe; but by August 13th, the column had forced a way through and the E.A.M.R. were trying their skill at bridge building at the back of Turiani, having again joined up with the 1st Division Headquarters. It may be of interest to give some account of the doings of the E.A.M.R. during the long halt at Tulo between September the 8th and November 8th, 1916.

It would have broken the heart of a thrifty General Manager of Railways to see what damage the Germans had done to their Central Railway in order that the British forces might not make use of the rolling stock and line. Bridges over ravines and river beds had been blown up, and then apparently trains had been started off at full speed to leap into the yawning chasms. The spectacle provided by such a happening would doubtless have filled a small boy's heart with joy, but the resulting wreckage was a melancholy sight to hungry soldiers expecting food to come along that line and realising that belts would have to be tightened, since the base on the Tanga line was now too far away to be of use and hungry days loomed ahead.

Already on August 31st food searching parties were sent out to gather in maize, rice, etc., and for the next two months the E.A.M.R. became a combination of Supply Corps, Military Labour Bureau and lines of communication troops, with its base at a lovely spot in the Uluguru Hills near Matombo.

The Uluguru Mountains were fairly thickly populated and the chiefs and headmen were called together to supply what labour was procurable. It was arranged to build certain grass depots where food could be brought and purchased from the natives, and when a drum signal from the E.A.M.R. camp sounded each chief would send in a given quota of porters to carry on loads to Tulo and elsewhere. This plan worked well and when rations began to come through it was not uncommon for 700 porters to be ready and waiting to carry loads where cars and other wheeled transport could not pass.

At about this time the weary, ragged and hungry South African Troops, infantry and mounted, which had taken part in this phase of the campaign, were passing back to the Railway. About this time too General Smuts left, having overrun a large area and captured the Railway and chief towns. But von Lettow and the greater part of his command was still at large, and many a bitter struggle was to come before he was eventually driven from German territory to carry on in Portuguese territory until the Armistice in Europe brought hostilities to a close.

One last glimpse. The E.A.M.R. had dwindled from a Regiment to a Squadron, from a Squadron to a Troop, from a Troop to one officer and four men, still carrying on with the advance as a unit.

It was at Muhoro, a port on the Rufiji River, that orders were received from G.H.Q. at Dar es Salaam "You will endeavour to get in touch and make contact with the Navy on the Rufiji".

"Well," remarked the Officer Commanding the four men, "here is a unit where we cannot expect to find any of the old E.A.M.R".

Contact was made; a boat from the monitor "Mersey" came up from the delta of the river to the port. The first man to leap ashore from the naval boat and salute the remnants of his old Regiment was one-time Trooper, Corporal, Sergeant, Lieutenant and now Captain Wreford Smith, temporarily attached for service in East African waters with the Royal Navy!

Appendix C
Important Dates in the History of the East African Mounted Rifles

1914

August	5	Enrolment commenced.
"	7	Mobile column in readiness.
"	15	Regiment inspected by H. E. the Governor and Commander-in-Chief.
"	30	"B" & "E" Squadrons left Nairobi for Kajiado and Kiu.
September	8	Regiment left Nairobi for Kajiado.
"	14	"B" & "E" Squadron left Kajiado for Kisumu.
"	15	Engagement at Karungu Bay.
"	25	Engagement at Ngito Hills.
October	29	Regiment moved to Namanga.
November	3	Battle of Longido.
"	17	Longido occupied.
"	25	Indefinite leave arranged.

1915

January	16	"D" Squadron left.
February	25	"B" and "E" Squadron lost their horses.

April	1	Regiment moved back to Bissil.
May	13	Seki water-hole patrol ambushed.
August	2	German patrol captured at Longido West.
Sept.	21	Engagement at Longido West.

1916

January	17	Regiment left Bissil for Longido.
"	19	Ambush at "Scatter Corner".
"	20	Regiment arrived Longido West.
March	5	Regiment left Longido West in General Advance.
"	10	Engagement at Geraragua.
"	16	Arrived Moshi.
"	20	Night attack at Store Camp.
"	24	Regiment arrived Arusha.
April	20	Regiment left Arusha.
"	26	Regiment arrived Kajiado.
"	28	Regiment arrived Mbuyuni.
May	20	Squadron left Mbuyuni.
June	24	Engagement at Lukigura River.
July		At Shell Camp.
August	5	Left Shell Camp.
"	12	Turiani.
"	20	Arrived Central Railway.

Appendix D
Nominal Roll

This list has been compiled as accurately as possible from all available Regimental and Squadron records. Date of joining the Regiment is that shown in Regimental Roll. In many cases date of enlistment may have been earlier. It is inevitable that there should be errors and omissions.

The following abbreviations have been used:-

E.A.M.S.	East African Medical Service.
E.A.P.C.	East African Pay Corps.
E.A.R.	East African Regiment.
E.A.S.C.	East African Supply Corps.
E.A.T.C.	East African Transport Corps.
I.D.	Intelligence Department.
K.A.R.	King's African Rifles.
M.L.C.	Military Labour Corps.
M.T.C.	Motor Transport Corps.

Name	Sqdn.	From	To	Remarks
Abraham, C.W.R.	E.	8/8/14	19/1/15	
Abrams, B.G.	E.	8/8/14	5/5/15	
Absalom, L.S.	D.	7/8/14	21/1/15	To E.A.T.C.
Absolom, J.L.	C.	26/6/15		Taken prisoner 21/9/15.
Acton, W.B.	E.	15/11/15		
Adams, A.W.	C.	10/ 9/14		L/Cpl. 12/10/14; Cpl. 5/1/15; Killed 21/9/15.
Adams, W.	A.	1/11/15		
Aggett, C.	E.	8/8/14	26/9/14	To E.A.T.C.
Aggett, C.G.	B.	12/1/15	27/4/15	From E.A.T.C.
Albrechtsen, O.W.	E.	20/8/14	9/3/15	To Scouts 12/12/14.
Aldous, R.	E.	8/8/14	14/9/14	
Allen, A.G.C.	C.	2/9/15		

Name	Sqdn.	From	To	Remarks
Allen, C.W.	A.	26/9/15		
Allen, H.	A.	16/9/15		From E.A.R.;Sergt. D.D.A & Q.M.G.'s Office.
Allen, J.M.	E.	30/1/15		Cpl. 1/4/15; Sergt. 1/6/15
Allen, P. de V.	B.	8/8/14	25/2/15	Wounded 3/11/14.
Allen, T.	B.	8/8/14	20/10/14	
Allen, W.J	E.	15/1/15		From Ross's Scouts
Allison, W. A. C.	B.	8/8/14	27/4/15	Cpl. 26/9/14.
Allsopp, R.	A.	7/8/14	27/4/15	L/Cpl. 10/8/14; Cpl.29/8/14; Capt. 18/12/14.
Anderson, A.	B.	1/2/15		Wounded 21/9/15.
Anderson, R.W.	C.	26/1/15		
Andrews, W.D.	E.	8/8/14	26/10/14	To E.A.S.C.
Anstey, A.C.	A.	9/8/14	7/10/14	To Somali Scouts.
Armfield, R.L.	A.	29/8/14	29/12/14	
Armstrong, A.W.	C.	28/10/15		
Armstrong, B.D.	B.	15/2/15	21/2/16	To K.A.R.
Arnesen, H.	C.	11/8/14	27/4/15	To M.T. C.
Arnoldi, A.F.	D.	7/8/14	21/1/15	Capt. 10/8/14; to E. A.T.C.
Arnoldi, E.A.	A.	7/8/14	21/1/15	L/Cpl. 26/9/14.
Arnoldi, F.J.	D.	7/8/14	23/1/15	
Arnott, V.J.	C.	26/6/15		
Atherton, F.S.D.	B.	8/8/14	4/12/14	
Attwood, E.J.	B.	3/2/15		
Aubrey, G.C.	B.	11/10/15		
Ayre-Smith, O.	B.	14/9/14		Cpl. 6/2/15; to I.D.
Bailey, Hon. A..	C.	7/8/14		Lieut. 10/8/14; Capt. 9/11/14.
Baillie, A.A.	C.	14/9/14	27/4/15	Cpl. 26/9/14.
Bailie, A. B.H.	E.	8/8/14	11/11/14	Lieut. 10/8/14
Baillon, R.	E.	18/11/15		
Ball, G.D.	C.	29/9/15		To E.A.S.C.
Ball, R.W.	C.	9/1/15		To E.A.S.C.
Bampflyde, Hon. H. de B.	A.	7/8/14	27/4/15	To K.A.R.
Banks, D.D.	E.	8/8/14		To E.A.S.C.
Barclay, A.V.	A.	7/8/14		To K.A.R.
Barcroft, W.E.	E.	8/8/14	24/10/14	
Barker, W.E.	B.	19/8/14	11/2/15	
Barnard, J.H.	D.-C.	7/8/14	27/4/15	L/Cpl. 4/9/14.
Barnes, G.	A.	18/10/14	1/5/15	To I.D.
Barnes, J.	C.	12/8/14	4/1/15	L/Cpl. 22/8/14; Cpl. 26/8/14; to I.D. 4/1/15.
Barr, D.	B.	9/9/15		To E.A.S.C.
Barrett, E.	A.	5/11/15		
Bateman, G.H.	E.	12/1/15		Missing 25/2/15.
Battersby, J.R.	B.	20/10/14		To Scouts; Cpl. 7/11/14; Sergt. 1/5/15.
Beazley, J.H.	E.	8/8/14	1/12/14	To E.A.V.C.
Beeston, J.	B.	8/8/14	29/4/15	
Bell, L.	C.	6/8/14	27/4/15	
Bell, L.C.	B.	8/8/14	18/2/15	
Bell, P.	D.	27/8/14	21/1/15	To E.A.T.C.
Bellasis, W.G.	B.	8/8/14		Killed 3/11/14.
Bellasis, R.F.	A.	6/11/15		To K.A.R.
Benham, J.H.F.	A.	2/9/14	19/11/14	
Bennett, A.H.	F.	10/8/14	4/10/14	
Bennett, G.W.	C.	9/8/14	1/12/14	L/Cpl. 10/8/14.
Bennett, P. S.	A.	7/8/14		To Signals.
Bentley, G.H.	B.	15/10/15		

Name	Sqdn.	From	To	Remarks
Bentley, T.W.	E.	9/9/14	27/4/15	
Bestall, F.J.	E.	18/9/14		
Bezuidenhout, J.M.	D.	10/8/14	21/1/15	To E.A.T.C.
Billingham, W.B.	F.	10/8/14	24/8/14	
Billiter, C.R.	A.	7/9/14	25/1/15	Sergt. 2/11/14; to M.T.C.
Bingley, A.E.	E.	8/8/14	15/7/15	Capt. 10/8/14; Major & Second in Command 9/11/14.
Bingley, A.R.	E.	8/8/14	27/4/15	To K.A.R
Bishop, G.A.	B.	25/1/15		
Blain, B.M.	A.	17/10/14	4/7/15	
Blain, W.	B.	8/8/14	27/4/15	
Blanc, M.	A.	17/10/14	4/7/15	To M.G.S.
Boardman, P.D.	E.	15/1/15		To E.A.S.C.
Botha, C.R.	E.	15/1/15		
Botha J.J.	D.	27/8/14	23/10/14	
Botha, S.J.	D.	27/8/14	30/12/14	
Bourke, U.H.	M.G.S.	7/8/14	19/1/15	To E.A.R.
Bouwers, G.R.	A.	26/8/14	25/3/15	
Bowden, A.G.	B.	8/8/14		
Bowker, Russell	B.	5/8/14	29/10/14	Capt. 5/8/14.
Bradbury, J.	E.		18/2/15	
Bradish, F.	E.	8/8/14	27/4/15	
Bradshaw, J.T.C.				Capt. E.A.V.C. Attchd.
Braithwaite, A.		5/8/14	18/8/14	Capt.
Brampton, J.R.C.	A.	26/11/14		To M.G.S.
Bramwell, F.	M.G.S.	8/8/14		
Bramwell, W.D.	A.	1/11/15		
Branitzky, S.	A.	6/8/14	3/5/15	
Brebner, J.H.	C.	8/8/14	27/4/15	
Brick, T.	M.G.S.	8/8/14		To K.A.R.
Brine, J.E.	A.	11/8/14	11/5/15	
Brinkworth, E.A.	E.	8/8/14	23/10/14	
Broom, L.J.	E.	14/9/14		L/Cpl. 4/11/14; Sergt. 24/1/15; S.S.M.11/5/15.
Brown, C.J.	E.	14/8/14		To Scouts.
Brown, J.	B.	8/8/14	16/3/15	To Signals 22/9/14.
Brown, J.G.	B.	7/10/15		
Brown, Q.H.	C.	8/8/14	9/11/14	To E.A.T.C.
Brown, T.	E.			L/Cpl. 21/11/14.
Brown, T.H.	C.	10/8/14	12/10/14	L/Cpl. 26/9/14; to K.A.R.
Brummage, D.	B.	8/8/14	17/11/14	
Bruno, C.	M.G.S.		Lieut. 21/10/14.	
Buchanan, R.G.	E.	21/9/14	10/12/14	To Police Mil. Service Battn.
Buller, F.E.	C.	7/8/14		Killed 25/9/14.
Buller, J.F.	A.	30/10/15	To K.A.R.	
Burch, D.	E.	8/8/14	18/11/14	
Burden, G.G.	E.	13/2/15		
Burmeister, F.L.	E.	8/8/14		Staff Sergt. 6/11/14; to Force Amm. Col.
Burnell, P.H.	C.	9/9/14	17/12/14	To Scouts.
Burnham, F.H.	B.	12/1/15		
Burridge, A.C.	C.	7/8/14		L/Cpl. 10/8/14; killed 25/ 9/14.
Burt, W.G.	C.	27/9/14		
Butler, C.W.L.	A.	7/8/14		
Butler, R.H.T.	B.	25/1/15		
Butler, I.C.	C.	15/9/15		

Name	Sqdn.	From	To	Remarks
Button, J.C.	C.	15/9/15		
Cable, H.R.	C.	19/8/14		
Caine, W. H.	E.	6/3/15		
Cameron, J.	C.	9/11/14	22/11/14	To E.A.T.C.
Cameron, J.H.	M.G.S.	8/8/14	20/2/15	To E.A.V.C.
Campell, W.W.		3/3/16		
Campling, F.K.	C.	6/8/14		To Signals: Cpl. 15/ 5/16; to K.A.R.
Carey, H.D.T.	C.	14/9/14	29/10/15	To K.A.R.
Carpena, A.W.	E.	14/12/15		
Carson, A.H.	C.	11/9/14	24/10/14	
Cartwright, A.R.	A.	14/9/14	27/4/15	
Catchpole, G.	A.	10/8/14	1/5/15	To I.D.
Chambers, F.T.	A.	5/8/14	14/2/15	Sergt. 10/8/14; S.S.M. 26/9/14; to Home Regt.
Chapman, P.	C.	7/8/14	11/11/14	Capt. 11/8/14.
Charrington, S.H.	Sigs.	6/8/14		Capt. 10/8/14; retd. to Eng.
Cheshire, J.B.	D.-A.	31/8/14		Medical Orderly 1/10/14.
Chivell, R.L.	C.	27/8/14	14/11/14	To E.A.T.C.
Chorley, C.C.	E.	9/3/15		Wounded 19/1/16.
Church, A.	E.	22/1/15		To I.D.
Clair, W.	C.	14/9/14	10/6/15	To Scouts 22/10/14.
Clarey, C.	E.	15/1/15	3/5/15	From Ross's Scouts.
Clarke, H.W.	B.	11/10/15		
Clarke, J.	E.	8/8/14		
Clarke, P.H.	C.	9/8/14	14/9/15	
Claydon, A.W.R.	E.	8/8/14		L/Cpl. 10/8/14; Cpl. 26/9/14; to Scouts.
Cleverly, J.W.G.	C.	6/11/15		
Cloete, S.W	D.	9/8/14	21/1/15	L/Cpl. 26/9/14; to E.A.T.C.
Clothier				Farrier Sergt.
Cobham, E.	A.	5/8/14	27/4/15	L/Cpl. 10/8/14; Cpl. 2/9/14; Chaplain
Cole, A.T.		10/8/14	9/11/14	Capt.
Colliver, A.H.	A.	2/9/14		L/Cpl. 18/12/14; Cpl. 1/11/15; Sergt. 6/12/15; to K.A.R.
Coleman-Brown, E.A.		2/9/14	27/4/15	L/Cpl. 2/9/14; to K.A.R.
Coltart, H.C.	B.	16/10/15		To M.L.C.
Compton, S.	C.	24/9/14		
Connor, T.	E.-B.	15/1/15	3/5/15	From Ross's Scouts.
Conybeare, C.B.	A.	13/9/14	16/11/14	Re-enlisted 26/10/15.
Cooke, A.	E.	8/8/14	27/4/15	
Cooke, J.	E.	26/9/15		
Cooper, A.	E.	29/11/15		
Cooper, P.H.	E.	23/4/15		
Cowling, J.	E.	7/10/15		To E.A.S.C.
Cramer, P.J.	M.G.S.	7/9/14		Armourer Sergt. 8/11/14
Craven, A.E.L.	A.	15/9/14	9/8/15	
Crawford, F.L.	C.	6/8/14		To E.A.S.C.
Crawford, G.	A.	8/8/14		Cpl. 6/12/16; to E.A.S.C.
Crawford, T.	A.	8/8/14		
Cripps, A.E.	C.	7/8/14	19/8/14	

Name	Sqdn.	From	To	Remarks
Cunningham, A.	A.	7/9/14	28/9/14	
Curnow, S.J.D.	B.	25/10/15		
Curry, C.D.	E.	14/9/14	5/3/15	
Curtis, J.F.S.	M.G.S.	7/10/15		
Dakin, J.E.H.	E.	8/8/14	30/11/14	L/Cpl. 10/8/14.
Danziger, H.	B.	26/1/15	27/4/15	
Dansie, C.	C.	27/10/15		To K.A.R.
Dare, C.M.	B.	8/8/14	27/3/15	
Davis, C.	A.	24/11/15		
Davis, F.	C.	26/9/14	22/3/15	To E.A.P.C.
Davies-Evans, A.	A.	2/9/14	27/4/15	L/Cpl. 2/9/14; Cpl. 26/9/14.
Dawson, C.C.	A.	7/8/14		L/Cpl. 6/12/15; to K.A.R.
Dawson, J.	E.	25/1/15		Killed 13/5/15.
Dawson, H.C.	A.	7/8/14	11/5/15	To K.A.R.
Dawson, W.J.	B.	8/8/14	13/10/14	Cpl. 10/8/14; to E.A.V.C
Deakin, R.H.	E.	28/10/14		
De Cerjat, F.	B.	10/8/14		Killed 3/11/14.
De Jager, F.J.	D.	7/8/14	5/1/15	
De Jager, P.J.L.C.	D.	7/8/14	21/1/15	To E.A.T.C.
De Waal, E.H.	D.	7/8/14		L/Cpl. 26/9/14.
Dedonkele, R.R.	E.	28/11/14		Killed 19/1/16.
Dennis, J.G.	B.	26/10/14		To Scouts; wounded; taken prisoner 21/9/15.
Dent, C.	E.	8/8/14	26/9/14	To K.A.R.
Dent, R.G.	B.	8/8/14	15/9/14	To K.A.R.
Dickens, W.H.	C.	12/2/15		To E.A.S.C.
Dobbie, H.	B.	19/10/15		To E.A.T.C.
Dobbin, H.W.L.	B.	27/1/15	27/4/15	
Doble, F. J.	E.	8/8/14	12/12/14	
Doherty, H.S.	C.	6/3/15		
Donnelly, S.	B.	8/8/14	29/8/14	
Douglas, A.	C.		9/11/14	To E.A.T.C.
Douglas, W.	B.	9/9/15		To E.A.S.C.
Douglass, F.W.	B.	26/10/14		Lieut. 15/11/14; Capt.1/2/15.
Dovey, G.C.	C.	6/8/14		To Scouts.
Drake, T.H.	B.	8/8/14		Killed 3/11/14.
Driscoll, B.O.		31/8/14		
Drought, J.J.	E.	15/1/15		Lieut; from Ross's Scouts; Capt. 1/9/15.
Drummond, F.G.	B.	8/8/14		Killed 3/11/14.
Drury, N.C.	B.	15/11/15		
Dry, T.A.	D.	27/8/14	21/1/15	To E.A.T.C.
Dry, G.C.	D.	27/8/14	21/1/15	To E.A.T.C.
Ducrotoy, P.	E.	11/2/15	6/12/15	Wounded 13/5/15; to E.A.M.S.
Duffy, J.F.	B.	25/8/14	24/10/14	
Duirs, A.B.	B.	5/8/14	1/2/15	Lieut. 8/8/14; Capt. 30/10/14.
Duirs, E.G.	E.	8/8/14		to Scouts.
Dunman, V.W.	B.	8/8/14		Cpl. 10/8/14; Sergt. 21/11/14; Lieut. 6/12/15; to K.A.R.
Dunn, A.H.	C.	7/8/14		
Du Plessis, N.J.	A.	24/9/15		
Du Preez, I.J.	D.	13/8/14	24/12/14	To E.A.T.C.
Du Toit, J.J.	D.	7/8/14	21/1/15	To E.A.T.C.
Eadie, C.G.	B.	19/10/15		To M.L.C.

Name	Sqdn.	From	To	Remarks
Eames, L.F.	A.	24/11/14		
Eardley, W.	A.	23/9/15		M.G.S. 19/10/15.
Eardley, W.W.	A.	4/9/15	27/9/15	To K.A.R.
Edmunds, S.F.	C.			Killed 25/9/14.
Edwards, W.G.	A.	7/8/14	27/4/15	To K.A.R.
Elliot, F.M.	E.	15/1/15		From Ross's Scouts.
Elliott, L.J.	C.	7/8/14		Killed 25/9/14.
Englebrecht, J.M.	D.	7/8/14	21/5/15	To E.A.T.C.
Englebrecht, J.P.	D.	7/8/14	1/12/14	Sergt. 10/8/14; S.S.M. 26/9/14.
Englebrecht, J.P.	A.	10/8/14	20/12/15	Sergt. 20/8/14.
Evans, E.A.S.	C.	8/8/14	27/4/15	To K.A.R.
Evans, W.J.	E.	8/8/14		Cpl. 10/8/14; Sergt. 1/12/14.
Evans, L.F.	C.	7/8/14	18/11/14	L/Cpl. 10/8/14; wounded 25/9/14; to Loyal N.Lancs.
Evans, S.	B.	8/8/14	25/1/15	
Farrer, F.L.	A.	2/9/14		Cpl. 2/9/14; Sergt. 26/9/14; Lieut. 6/1/15.
Farrow, F.H.	B.	3/3/15		To K.A.R.
Fenwick, P.	E.	15/1/15	26/1/15	
Fielden, C.M.	A.	20/8/14		Cpl. 14/12/14
Findlay, H.C.	M.G.S.	7/9/14		To K.A.R.
Findlay, K.J.	M.G.S.	7/9/14	8/6/15	To K.A.R.
Fitzgerald, C.B.P.	B.	8/8/14	18/11/14	To Remounts.
Fitzgerald, H.G.	C.	9/3/15		
Fitzpatrick, G.	E.	18/8/15		
Fitzpatrick, P.W.	E.	25/5/15		
Flemmer, H.T.	A.	11/10/15		
Fletcher, F.	E.	8/8/14	28/8/14	
Flint, P.W.E.	A.	27/10/15		
Folkard, L.	B.	21/8/14	30/11/14	
Forbes, R.H.	E.	10/9/14	27/4/15	L/Cpl. 26/9/14.
Forgan, W.J.	A.	5/8/14	12/12/14	Cpl. 10/8/14; Sergt. 2/9/14.
Forester, A.C.	C.	10/9/14		Killed 25/9/14.
Foster, J.	B.	9/2/15		L/Cpl. 11/5/15.
Frank, L.S.M.	B.	8/8/14	12/1/15	To E.A.T.C.
Frazer, D.E.	A.	15/9/15		
Frederickson, R.	M.G.S.	5/9/14		L/Cpl. 28/11/14; Armourer Sergt. 12/5/15.
Friar, T.E.	A.	15/9/14	11/12/14	
Fry, A.S.	C.	5/1/15		
Fuller, B.J.	B.	8/8/14		
Furley, H.M.	E.	8/8/14		L/Cpl. 10/8/14; Cpl. 26/9/14; killed 3/11/14.
Gain, W.A.	E.		13/10/14	To E.A.T.C.
Galbraith, T.H.	A.	25/10/15		To Topograph. Sect.
Gale, J. F.E.	C.	8/8/14		Killed 28/1/15.
Gardner, H.M.	A.	1/11/15		
Garibaldi			9/12/14	
Garvie, L.	B.		28/9/14	
George, F.	E.	7/10/15		
George, W.E.	C.	17/9/14		Cpl. 17/12/14; Medical Orderly.
Germishuis, G.	A.	30/9/15		
Gibbs, N.M.	C.	9/9/14		Killed 20/9/16.
Gilbert, C.O.	E.	15/10/15		To Topograph. Sect.

Name	Sqdn.	From	To	Remarks
Gillilan, H.P.	A.	7/8/14	10/10/15	L/Cpl. 27/11/14; to K.A.R.
Gilson, J.F.	C.	8/8/14	2/11/14	
Gladwin, C.	D.	10/8/14	17/11/14	L/Cpl. 20/8/14; Cpl. 26/9/14; to E.A.T.C.
Gladwin, V.C.	D.	10/8/14	30/11/14	
Goldworthy, G.F.	B.	8/8/14	27/4/15	To K.A.R.
Gooch, E.D.A.	A.	20/8/14		Lieut. 20/8/14.
Goodson, R.	E.	8/8/14	24/8/14	
Gordon, C.F.	M.G.S.	11/11/15		
Gosling, J.E.	C.	3/10/14	25/11/14	To M.T.C.
Gould, H.C.	M.G.S.	20/2/15		L/Cpl. 1/9/15; Capt. 6/12/15.
Gould, L.A.	E.	29/9/14	22/6/15	Re-enlisted 22/12/15.
Grant, D.K.S.	C.	1/11/15	27/3/16	To K.A.R.
Gray, C.H.V.	E.-C.	15/1/15	1/5/15	From Ross's Scouts; to I.D.
Gray, H.J.C.	E.	2/9/15		
Gray, W.	C.	2/9/15		
Grazebrook, W.	B.	8/8/14	22/10/14	To E.A.S.C.
Greatham, C. G.	C.	9/9/14	4/11/14	
Greenslade, G.	E.	15/1/15	4/2/15	From Ross's Scouts; Sergt.
Grice, J.A.	B.	6/8/14	22/6/15	
Grieve, A.A.	B.	8/8/14	27/4/15	
Griffiths, G. G.	C.	29/9/14	31/3/15	L/Cpl. 19/11/14.
Grobler, N.J.	D.	19/8/14		To Scouts 22/10/14.
Groenewald, H.D.	E.	15/1/15	12/2/15	
Grogan, A.W.	E.	8/8/14		L/Cpl. 10/8/14.
Grove, G. E.	C.		1/11/14	L/Cpl. 10/8/14; to I.D.
Groves, D. J.	C.	4/1/15		To I.D. 1/5/15.
Guillauman, A.	E.	13/2/15		
Gunnell, A.H.	A.	10/8/14		L/Cpl. 19/8/14; Sergt. 7/1/15; S.S.M. 1/10/15.
Gunson, W.H.	A.	12/10/15		To K.A.R.
Guy, F.G.	C.	6/8/14		L/Cpl. 21/9/15; Cpl. 21/10/15.
Hall, C.O.	A.	4/12/15		
Hall, T.H.	C.	6/8/14	9/11/14	To E.A.T.C.
Hall, W	E.	14/9/14	13/10/14	
Hamilton, J.	E.	8/8/14		
Hamilton, T.W.	E.	5/8/14	22/11/14	To E.A.T.C.
Hampson, G.	M.G.S.	7/8/14	1/3/15	Lieut.
Handley, I.	A.	2/9/14	10/12/14	To E.A. Police Mil.Battn.
Hanmer, E.	C.		18/8/14	
Harcombe, J.H.	A.	29/9/15		To E.A.S.C.
Hards, T.C.	A.	2/9/14	19/10/14	To E.A.S.C.
Harger, R.I.	A.	2/9/14	1/1/15	
Harper, P.	E.	7/10/15		
Harries, A.I.R.	B.	8/8/14	10/5/15	Cpl. 16/9/14; wounded 3/11/14; to R.E. Ry. Corps.
Harries, O.C.	E.	8/8/14	18/1/15	Cpl. 10/8/14; Sergt.26/9/14.
Harris, H.R.	C.		9/11/14	To E.A.T.C.
Hartley, C.	A.	7/8/14	19/1/15	L/Cpl. 10/8/14.
Harvey, C.	C.	9/9/14	27/4/15	Sergt. 5/10/14.
Harvey, H.	C.	9/9/14		To E.A.S.C.
Hawkins, L.	C.	14/9/14		To Scouts 19/6/15; Cpl. 4/9/15; Sergt.9/11/15; to K.A.R.

Name	Sqdn.	From	To	Remarks
Hawkins, W.G.	A.	3/11/15		
Haywood, C.W.	A.	2/9/14	1/10/14	Cpl. 10/9/14; to Somali Scouts.
Heard, P.R.H.J.	C.	22/10/15		
Heath, W.A.	M.G.S.	10/8/14		
Heaton, P. R.	E.	8/8/14		Awarded D.C.M.
Henderson, R.G.	A.	18/12/15		
Hennessy, E.J.	C.	3/9/15		
Herring, C.S.W.	B.	9/8/14		
Hervey, C.G.	E.	8/8/14	27/4/15	
Hessletine	C.	28/10/14	11/12/14	To Scouts.
Hewitson, H.	E.	18/2/15		
Hewitt, G.	C.	6/8/14	1/12/14	To Signals 22/9/14; to K.A.R.
Hewitt, J.G.	M.G.S.	10/8/14	20/10/14	
Hignell, H.	C.	14/9/14	27/4/15	To E.A.P.C.
Hill, C.A.	C.	12/9/14		Lieut. 12/9/14; Capt. 1/11/14; Major 10/11/15; Officer Commanding.
Hill, R.C.	M.G.S.	7/8/14		Sergt. 7/8/14; Lieut 26/11/14; Capt; wounded 10/3/16.
Hill, T.R.	C.	6/11/15		
Hill, W.	B.	1/11/15		
Hillier, R.G.	E.	4/10/15		
Hillyer, M.	E.	15/1/15	13/2/15	Sergt; from Ross's Scouts.
Hilton, C.K.	C.	10/9/14		L/Cpl. 5/1/15; wounded; taken prisoner 21/9/15.
Hoddinott, B.R.	A.	7/8/14		
Hoddinott, R.W.		8/3/16		
Hodgkinson, G.W.	A.	5/8/14	6/1/15	Lieut. 10/8/14.
Hoey, A.E.	M.G.S.	1/12/15		
Hoey, W. H.	C.	6/8/14	27/4/15	To Signals 22/9/14; Sergt. 24/9/14.
Holgate, J. B.	E.	2/9/15		
Holland, G.	E	.8/8/14	13/10/14	
Holland, H. de la P.	C.	25/10/15		To E.A.S.C.
Holmberg, E.	M.G.S.	10/8/14	14/11/14	L/Cpl. 14/9/14.
Holzapfel, J.W.	E.	8/8/14	22/4/15	To E.A.M.S.
Homewood, R.	B.	8/8/14	3/3/15	
Hopcraft, J.D.	A.		17/8/14	
Hoult, G.A.	A.	1/11/15		
House, T.F.	B.	8/8/14		
Howard, M.	A.	26/8/15		To M.G.S. 28/10/15.
Howitt, CA.	C.	19/8/14	27/4/15	Cpl. 18/11/14.
Hudson, E.E.C.	C.	16/8/15		To Administration.
Humphreys, S.	E.	8/8/14	26/8/14	
Hunt, D.A.	M.G.S.	19/8/14		To Scouts 5/1/15.
Hunter, P.H.R.	A.	13/10/15		
Hurst, G.H.R.	C.	10/9/14		Cpl. 14/9/14; Sergt. 10/11/14; Lieut.25/11/14; to Gen. Staff.
Hutchinson, E.	A.	8/8/14	1/11/14	Cpl. 10/8/14; Sergt. 29/8/14; S.Q.M.S.
Hutchins, E.E.	M.G.S.	26/1/15		To Administration.
Hutson, W.	B.	8/8/14	27/10/14	Sergt. 10/8/14.
Ievors, H.W.	A.	10/9/14		

Name	Sqdn.	From	To	Remarks
Imbert, A.E.T.	E.		23/9/14	Sergt. 10/8/14; to E.A.T.C.
Impey, A.D.	B.	8/8/14		Cpl. 26/9/14; Sergt. 6/12/15; to E.A.S.C.
Impey, A.T.	C.	8/8/14		L/Cpl. 22/8/14; killed 25/9/14.
Isherwood, J.	B.	8/8/14	27/4/15	To E.A.P.C. as Pay Sergt.
Jackson, G.V.	C.	7/4/15		Taken prisoner 21/ 9/15; later to E.A.S.C.
Jacobson, D.M.	E.	7/12/15		
Jameson, F. O.	B.	25/4/15		M.G.S.; to K.A.R.
Jenkins, O.J.	B.	18/1/15		L/Cpl; to Scouts.
Jessel, V.F.G.	C.	4/1/15		
Johnston, C.C.	C.	29/10/15		To K.A.R.
Johnston, C.W.	M.G.S.	11/11/15		
Johnston, W.K.	B.	19/10/15		To E.A.S.C.
Jolley, C.B.	B.	10/8/14		
Jones, D.T.	E.	8/8/14	13/11/14	
Jordan, F.H.	A.	3/2/15	10/10/14	To Ordnance.
This is as appears in original text, perhaps the dates have been transposed				
Joubert, J.J.	D.	16/8/14	30/12/14	To E.A.T.C.
Joubert, L.M.	A.	4/10/15		
Joubert, M.	D.	7/8/14	21/1/15	L/Cpl. 26/9/14; to E.A.T.C.
Joubert, M. (Jnr.)	D.	2/12/14	30/12/14	To E.A.T.C.
Joubert, M.G.	D.	16/8/14	30/12/14	To E.A.T.C.
Joubert, P.C.	D.	7/8/14	21/1/15	Lieut. 10/8/14; to E.A.T.C.
Joubert, W.P.	D.	16/8/14	4/12/14	To E.A.T.C.
Jowers, J.	A.	5/8/14	19/19/14	To Ordnance.
Joyce, F.H. de V.	A.	5/8/14		Lieut. 22/8/14; to R.F.A.
Kay-Mouat, E.W.	B.	8/8/14		Killed 3/11/14.
Keightley-Smith, B.	A.	24/11/14		
Keith, J.	E.	4/9/15		
Kemp, J.	C.	7/8/14		7/12/14 Sergt. 19/8/14.
Kenealy, E.M.V.	C.	14/8/14		L.Cpl. 1/12/14; Cpl. 16/7/15; to K.A.R.
Kennett, J. H. Barrington	C.	16/1/15		From Ross's Scouts.
Kerr, F.W.	E.	8/8/14	1/10/14	
Kilian, C.J.	F.	10/8/14	19/10/14	To E.A.T.C.
Kilian, J.D.	F.	10/8/14	19/10/14	To E.A.T.C.
Kilian, J.G.	F.	10/8/14	20/10/14	Re-enlisted 15/1/15
Kirk, H.J.	B.	19/1/15		
Klopper, J.J.	D.	7/8/14	1/12/14	Re-enlisted 4/10/15.
Klopper, P.J.	D.	27/8/14	21/1/15	To E.A.T.C.
Klynsmith, D.C.	D.	8/8/14	21/1/15	Cpl. 26/9/14.
Knobel, L.J.	F.			Lieut. 20/8/14; Base Commandant, Kajiado.
Knobel, T.W.	F.	10/8/14	4/9/14	
Knox, J.K.G.	B.	26/1/15	10/8/15	To 17th Cavalry.
Kruger, P.I.J.	D.	7/8/14	21/1/15	To E.A.T.C.
Laing, G.J.	E.	7/10/15		
Laing, H.D.	E.	7/10/15		
Lambert, H.	A.	5/8/14	19/3/15	To Signals & K.A.R.
Lane, R.	B.	1/2/15	18/10/15	

Name	Sqdn.	From	To	Remarks
Langhaen, J.	D.	7/8/14	25/11/14	To E.A.T.C.
Laverton, H.S.		10/8/14		Capt. 10/8/14; Major; Officer Commanding 9/11/14; Lt.-Col 10/11/15.
Lawrence, L.E.	A.	8/8/14	29/8/14	To M.T.C.
Laws, E. L.	A.	6/1/15		L/Cpl. 3/10/15.
Laws, H. R.	E.	23/12/14		L/Cpl. 1/4/15.
Leach, R.W. H.	C.	9/9/14		
Le Breton, J.G.	A.	8/8/14	29/4/15	To K.A.R.
Leka, A.	C.	7/4/15		
Lekander, E.	C.	24/8/15		
Le May, L.H.	B.	7/8/14		L/Cpl. 27/10/14; wounded & taken prisoner 10/3/16.
Le Page, H.	D.	27/8/14		Mauled by lion; died 30/10/14.
Le Roux, J.P.	D.	7/8/14	3/9/14	L/Cpl. 10/8/14.
Lester, G.F.	C.	25/1/15		
Levinson, B.	C.	8/8/14		To M.G.S. 19/10/15.
Lewis, C. J.	C.	25/2/15	27/4/15	To Scouts.
Lind, F.V.	A.	24/12/15		
Lindsay, E.L.	A.	15/8/14	29/4/15	To K.A.R.
Linnell, F.	A.	18/9/14	23/10/14	
Little, A. M.			15/8/14	To 2nd L.of D.
Lloyd, E.	B.	8/8/14		L/Cpl. 24/9/14; Sergt. & S.S.M. 1/11/14.
Lloyd, J. J.	E.	14/6/15		
Lloyd, W. G.	B.	11/6/15		
Logan, J.	M.G.S.	8/8/14	27/10/14	
Logan, J.	E.	15/1/15		Sergt; from Ross's Scouts.
Lombard, T. G.	D.	10/8/14	28/12/14	Cpl. 20/8/14; to E.A.T.C.
Loveridge, A.	E.	27/12/15		
Lunan, D. C.	E.	8/8/14		S.S.M. 26/9/14; wounded 3/11/14.
Lunan, R.	B.	8/8/14	26/10/14	L/Cpl. 10/8/14; to E.A.S.C.
Lushington, E.G.	A.	11/9/14	12/11/14	
Lydford, H.C.	C.	2/12/15		
Lydford, S.T.	B.	25/2/15		
MacDonald, B.	B.	18/8/15		Signaller.
MacDonald, C. R.	A.		16/11/14	Attchd. E.A.M.R. from Behar Light Horse.
McDonogh, J.E.				Sergt. E.A.M.S. (attchd.)
Maclean, H.	D.	7/8/14	30/11/14	L/Cpl. 10/8/14; Cpl. 26/9/14; to I.D.
Mandy, A.F.	B.	7/10/15		Killed 21/3/16.
Manley, J.F.	A.	5/8/14	14/12/14	L/Cpl. 10/8/14; Cpl. 26/9/14.
Mann, O.A.	D.	9/8/14	21/1/15	L/Cpl. 10/8/14; Cpl. 26/9/14; to E.A.T.C.
Manning, A.C.	E.	8/8/14	21/11/14	L/Cpl. 10/8/14; Cpl. 15/9/14.
Maree, J.	C.	9/3/15		
Marquordt, F.A.F.	B.	7/9/14	28/12/14	To M.T.C.
Marshall, H.B.	C.	9/11/14		
Martin, A.E.	B.	10/8/14		
Martin, G.	B.	8/2/15		
Matthews, S.L.	A.	7/8/14	4/1/15	To E.A.V.C.

Name	Sqdn.	From	To	Remarks
Mayne, A.E.	A.	11/10/15		
McAllister, A.	C.	7/9/14	27/4/15	Cpl. 13/8/14.
McCallum, A.H.	F.	13/8/14	29/10/14	L/Cpl. 20/8/14.
McClelland, R.	E.	15/1/15	1/6/15	To M.L.C.
McClure, E.R.	E.	15/1/15		L/Cpl. 25/1/15; Cpl. 2/3/15.
McDonald, F.	E.	7/7/15		
McDonnell, A.B.	C.	14/9/14	19/12/14	
McGeorge, R.				Sergt. E.A.M.S. (attchd.)
McGregor, D.	E.	7/7/15		To E.A.S.C.
McKenzie, C.	C.	2/9/15		
McMahon, P.		30/10/15		
McMillan, C.	C.	25/8/15		Killed 21/9/15.
Mercer, M.	E.	8/8/14		L/Cpl. 15/9/14; Cpl. 26/9/14; Sergt. 11/1/15; S.S.M. 23/1/15.
Middlemass, T.P.	B.	18/10/15		
Middleton, C.M.	C.	6/8/14		L/Cpl. 10/8/14; Cpl. 19/11/14; Sergt. 6/12/15; to E.A.S.C.
Middleton, J.B.	C.	6/3/15		To Scouts.
Miles, A.T.	A.	20/8/14	1/10/14	To Somali Scouts.
Millett, G.C.		10/8/14	13/8/14	Lieut. 10/8/14; to Town Guard.
Milligan, J.W.		5/8/14	15/5/16	Lieut. & Q.M. 10/8/14; Capt. 15/10/14; to E.A.S.C.
Milne, A.	C.	7/ 8/14	1/5/15	Farrier Sergt. 10/8/14; To E.A.V.C.
Misquith, J.C.	A.	7/8/14	14/1/15	
Mitchell, F.	E.	27/11/14		
Montagu, M.S.H.	A.	5/8/14		Lieut. 10/8/14; Capt. 9/11/14.
Moon, L.J.	B.	8/8/14		Killed 3/11/14.
Moore, C.G.L.	D.	9/8/14	21/1/15	Sergt. 1/12/14; to E.A.T.C.
Morgan, L.S.		4/3/16		
Mortimer, A.	E.	14/10/14	27/11/14	L/Cpl. 10/2/15.
Mortimer, J.A.	E.	15/1/15		
Morton, H. D.	D.	27/ 8/14	21/1/15	To E.A.T.C.
Mudie, R.M.	C.	14/9/14	4/12/14	To Kajiado Ammn. Col.
Mullen, J.C.O.	A.	5/9/14		
Muller, J. H.	D.	7/8/14	28/12/14	To E.A.T.C.
Mundell, J. McNab	C.	7/8/14		R.S.M. 10/8/14; Lieut. 30/10/15; to Administration.
Munro, R.W.	A.	7/8/14		L/Cpl. 10/8/14; to K.A.R. 19/8/14.
Murray, A.E.M.	E.			To Signals 22/9/14; L/Cpl. 21/12/15; to Administration.
Murray, L.B.	C.	7/9/14	1/5/15	To E.A.S.C.
Murray, T. J.	C.	14/8/14		L/Cpl. 21/10/15; Cpl. 6/12/15; to K.A.R.
Murrell, H. F.	C.	7/8/14		R.Q.M.S. 10/8/14; R.S.M. 21/10/15; to E.A.S.C.
Murrow, A. H.	C.	7/8/14	27/4/15	Saddler Sergt. 10/8/14.

Name	Sqdn.	From	To	Remarks
Murphy, J.	D.	27/8/14	21/1/15	To E.A.T.C.
Murphy, R.F.	E.	8/8/14	14/12/14	To M.T.C.
Murton, I.M.	C.	7/9/14	9/3/15	To E.A.V.C.
Muscatt, K.E.	C.	2/11/15		
Myers, J.	B.	8/8/14	26/10/14	
Nath, P.	E.	7/10/15		
Nesbitt, A.		2/ 9/14		To K.A.R.
Nesfield, W.	E.	12/8/14	15/2/15	To Signals 2/9/14; wounded 3/11/14.
New, E.G.	E.	8/8/14		Killed 19/1/16.
Neylan, D.N.	C.	9/9/14	9/1/15	
Nicholas, T.	M.G.S.	7/9/14	27/4/15	
Nielsen, S.	E.	22/5/15		To Scouts.
Nightingale, W.M.	B.	8/8/14	28/9/14	L/Cpl. 10/8/14; to E.A.T.C.
Noden, T.J.	E.	8/8/14		To Signals 22/9/14; Cpl. 1/12/14; Sergt.20/12/15.
Norman, G.B.	A.	12/8/14	27/4/15	
Nugent, G.	M.G.S.	14/9/14	19/11/14	
O'Beirne, A.J.L.	A.	2/9/14	3/5/15	
O'Brien, A.K.	A.	7/8/14		Capt. 11/8/14; to R.F.C.
O'Kelly, B.	E.	14/6/15		
Olivier, F.C.	D.	7/8/14	21/1/15	To E.A.T.C.
Olivier, J.C.	D.	7/8/14	4/1/15	
O'Meara, B.E.A.	B.	5/8/14		L/Cpl. 10/ 8/14; S.S.M. 24/10/14; Lieut. 1/11/14; wounded 3/11/14; to I.D.
Odendaal, F.J.	D.	7/8/14	21/1/15	To E.A.T.C.
Odendaal, J.B.	D.	7/8/14	29/12/14	To E.A.T.C.
Odendaal, S.J.	D.	7/8/14	21/1/15	To E.A.T.C.
Orchardson, G.Q.	M.G.S.	7/8/14	22/3/16	Sergt. 6/12/15; to K.A.R.
Otter, E.Von.	M.G.S.	7/8/14		Cpl. 7/8/14; to K.A.R.
Oxland, W. C.	C.	20/10/14		L/Cpl. 1/12/14; to K.A.R.
Pardoe, E.P.H.	C.	7/8/14	21/ 8/14	Lieut. 10/8/14; to K.A.R.
Parker, H.	E.	18/8/15		To Signals.
Parker, W.G.	E.	15/1/15		Lieut. Ross's Scouts.
Pasture, G.H. de la	A.	7/8/14	27/4/15	L/Cpl. 29/8/14; Cpl. 26/9/14; to K.A.R.
Paterson, A.	B.		24/3/15	To M.G.S. 31/10/14.
Patrick, T.W.	A.	10/8/14		L/Cpl. 2/9/14; Cpl. 26/9/14; Sergt. 1/11/15.
Patterson, G.	D.	10/8/14	21/1/15	To E.A.T.C.
Pearce, N.	E.	9/2/15		
Pears, R.C.	B.	8/8/14	15/5/15	
Pelham, D.V.	A.	7/8/14	18/12/14	L/Cpl. 29/8/14.
Pelham-Burn, R.	A.		9/9/14	To E.A.T.C.
Perks, G.	B.	1/2/15	1/5/15	To I.D.
Petrie, T.	B.	15/1/15		
Petter, H.St.A.	E.	1/10/14		
Pieterse, J.J.	F.	21/8/14	19/10/14	To E.A.T.C.
Pillieron, G.H.M.	B.	10/8/14	20/10/14	
Pixley, J.N.F.	A.	7/8/14	27/4/15	
Plenderleith, F.	C.	30/9/14		
Pohl, C.F.	D.	7/8/14	21/1/15	To E.A.T.C.
Pohl, L.	D.	7/8/142	1/1/15	To E.A.T.C.

Name	Sqdn.	From	To	Remarks
Potts, B.H.	A.	2/9/14	10/6/15	
Powell, W.C	E.	20/10/14		L/Cpl. 30/10/14; Cpl. 25/1/15.
Power, J.	B.	15/1/15	2/5/15	From Ross's Scouts.
Powys, W.E.	E.	5/2/15		L/Cpl. 1/9/15; to E.A.S.C.
Poy, C.J.S.	B.	25/8/14	27/4/15	
Poyer, L.P.	E.	20/2/15		Wounded 13/5/15
Pratt, E.R.	A.	25/10/15		
Pretorious, A.J.	D.	7/8/14	12/1/15	To E.A.T.C.
Pretorious, G.J.	D.	10/8/14		To Scouts 22/10/14; Cpl. 1/8/15; Sergt. 4/9/15; Lieut. 9/11/15.
Price, A.H.	C.	11/8/14		L/Cpl. 26/9/14; Cpl. 1/12/14; S.S.M.21/10/15.
Pridmore, L.	B.	8/8/14		Cpl. 22/1/15.
Priest, V.S.	E.	27/11/14	11/2/15	
Priestland, E.A.	B.	26/1/15		L/Cpl. 4/1/16; to K.A.R.
Prodgers, G.J.	B.	25/1/15		L/Cpl. 23/2/15; Cpl. 21/12/15; to E.A.S.C.
Rait, N.	A.	5/10/15		
Ramsey, S.H.	A.	15/11/15		
Randall, C.H.	B.-C.	2/2/15		
Ray, J.I.	B.	15/2/15	3/9/15	
Ray, M.S.	M.G.S.	11/9/14	24/12/14	
Redford, P.W.	C.	16/8/14		L/Cpl. 26/ 8/14; Cpl. 1/12/14.
Reichenbach, H.C.	A.	20/10/15		
Reid, G.E.H.	E.	14/9/14	19/12/14	L/Cpl. 5/10/14; to K.A.R.
Renton, S.	A.	12/10/15		To E.A.Pioneers.
Reynolds, G.A.	C.	7/4/15		To E.A.S.C.
Reynolds, G.W.	C.	7/8/14		L/Cpl. 3/5/15; Cpl. 22/9/15; to K.A.R.
Reynolds, R.	A.		1/9/14	L/Cpl. 10/8/14; to 2nd L. of D.
Ridley, M.A.	A.	2/9/14	7/12/14	
Ritchie, W.H.	A.	8/8/14	11/12/14	To M.TC.
Roach, P.E.	A.	21/8/14		L/Cpl. 2/9/14; Cpl. 8/12/14; Staff Sergt. 14/5/15.
Robbins W.J.	C.	9/11/14	22/11/14	To E.A.T.C.
Roberts, C.H.W.	M.G.S.	6/8/14		L/Cpl. 14/9/14; Sergt. 27/11/14; Lieut; to E.A.S.C.
Roberts, W.	C.	3/9/15		
Robertson, R.P.	C.	18/8/14	22/11/14	To E.A.T.C.
Robinson, C.	C.	7/8/14	9/11/14	To E.A.T.C.
Robinson, J.	E.	5/8/14	23/1/15	To Signals 22/9/14; Cpl. 1/10/14; to Mil.Tels.
Robinson, R.C.O.	E.-B.	15/1/15	2/5/15	From Ross's Scouts.
Robinson, R.F.	C.	26/6/15		
Rollnick, J.R.	A.	4/12/14	10/3/15	Re-enlisted
Ross, N.	E.	8/8/14	23/9/14	To E.A.T.C.
Rosslein, E.T.	F.	10/8/14	20/10/14	Cpl. 20/8/14.
Rowles, S.J.	B.	6/3/15		
Russell, T.	A.	11/9/14	3/11/14	
Sale, A.G.	C.	29/8/14	1/9/14	To E.A. Pioneers.

Name	Sqdn.	From	To	Remarks
Salkeld, G.	E.	28/10/14		Cpl; to Scouts; to E.A.T.C.
Sandbach, H.H.		5/8/14		Officer Commanding; Capt. 5/8/14; killed 3/11/14.
Saul, W.B.	B.	8/8/14	15/9/14	L/Cpl. 10/8/14.
Saunders, C.L.	B.	11/8/14		Cpl. 26/9/14; Sergt. 28/10/14; to Scouts.
Scally, J.J.	C.	8\8/14		Q.M.S. 10/8/14; S.S.M. 26/9/14; Lieut. 6/12/15; R.T.O.
Scanlen, J.R.C.	C.	21/1/15	29/4/15	To M.G.S.
Scanlen, F.J.	B.			Lieut. 20/8/14; A.P.M., Kajiado, 13/3/15.
Schulte, C.I.	E.	15/1/15	3/2/15	Cpl.; from Ross's Scouts.
Schumyn, C.A.	D.	7/8/14	21/1/15	To E.A.T.C.
Schweder, E.P.F.	B.	14/10/15		
Scott, C.	B.	7/10/15		
Scott, H.	E.		9/2/15	L/Cpl. 10/8/14.
Scott, J.	B.	8/6/15		
Scott, T.B.	E.	7/6/15		
Selby, J.H.	D.	10/8/14		Sergt. 10/8/14; Lieut. 9/11/14; to C. 21/1/15.
Sewall, W.G.	A.	30/8/14	19/12/14	
Shaw, F.C.	A.	14/8/14		Cpl. 1/11/14; wounded 3/11/14; to K.A.R.
Sheedy, F.J.				Capt. E.A.V.C. Attchd.
Sheen, C.	E.	8/8/14	31/8/14	
Sherrard, J.F.	A.	5/8/14		L/Cpl. 1/11/15; to K.A.R.
Sherwood, C.A.	B.	8/8/14		Killed 10/3/16.
Shipley, A.L.	B.	6/2/15		To M.G.S. 6/5/15.
Shipstone, R.F.	E.	2/9/15		
Shotton, F.G.	B.	8/8/14		To E.A.S.C.
Simpson, A.J.	C.	7/8/14	17/11/14	Sergt. 10/8/14.
Simpson, G.	B.	7/8/14		L/Cpl. 1/5/15; to K.A.R.
Simpson, J.H.	C.	27/9/14		Cpl. 6/12/15.
Sinclair, F.W.	B.	27/6/15		
Sizer, E.C.	B.	1/2/15		
Skewes-Cox, St. J.	A.	2/8/14	19/11/14	
Smart, A.T.	B.	8/8/14	28/9/14	
Smart, P.L.	C.	8/8/14		
Smit, C.J.	F.	12/8/14	20/10/14	To E.A.T.C.
Smit, J.C.	D.	7/8/14	31/10/14	
Smith, A.B.C.	E.	6/10/15		To E.A.S.C.
Smith, D.A.	C.	27/9/14	23/11/14	
Smith, G. le Blanc.	E.	8/8/14	10/12/14	L/Cpl. 4/11/14; awarded D.C.M.; to E.A. Police Mil. Battn.
Smith, H. Wreford	C.	7/8/14		Cpl. 10/8/14; Sergt. 18/11/14; Lieut; to I.D.
Smith, J.	A.	10/8/14		L/Cpl. 3/10/15; to Signals 14/10/15; Cpl. 1/11/15; to K.A.R.
Smith, O.A.	B.	14/9/14		

Name	Sqdn.	From	To	Remarks
Smith, R.J.	M.G.S.	7/8/14	11/3/15	L/Cpl. 10/8/14.
Smith, W.A.	E.	21/9/14		L/Cpl. 30/10/14; killed 3/11/14.
Smuts, J.O.	C.	11/9/15		
Sneque, C.A.	B.	21/8/14	11/12/14	
Soames, C.T.	E.	8/8/14	27/3/16	To K.A.R.
Somerville, W.F.	C.			Killed 25/9/14.
Southey, M.E.	C.	14/8/14	1/5/15	To Administration.
Squiers, J.G.	B.	8/8/14		L/Cpl. 10/8/14; Cpl. 1/5/15.
Stanley, C.A.	C.	7/8/14	1/3/15	
Stanning, C.G.	B.-C.	8/8/14		L/Cpl. 14/10/15; Cpl. 21/10/15; to E.A.S.C.
Stanton, A.A.	F.		20/8/14	To Town Guard.
Steenkamp, P.	D.	1/9/14	24/12/14	To E.A.T.C.
Stephen, R.	B.	8/8/14	28/8/14	To E.A.S.C.
Stephenson, P.	D.	12/8/14	4/1/15	
Stevens, L.A.V.	E.	8/8/14	22/11/14	To E.A.T.C.
Steyn, A.J.	E.	15/1/15		From Ross's Scouts.
Steyn, E.L.	D.	7/8/14	28/9/14	Cpl. 10/8/14.
Steyn, P.H.	D.	7/8/14	21/1/15	To E.A.T.C.
Stock, R.	B.	20/12/15		
Storey, R.C.	E.	15/1/15		From Ross's Scouts.
Stradling, C.A.	C.	7/8/14		Cpl. 10/8/14; Sergt. 7/12/14; S.S.M. 6/12/15.
Street, T.R.	E.	15/8/14	25/9/14	To E.A.M.S.
Stuttaford, P.C.	M.G.S.	16/10/15		
Sutherland, T.C.	E.	15/1/15		Sergt.; from Ross's Scouts.
Sutton, G.J.	C.	5/11/15		To E.A.S.C.
Swart, P.L.	D.-C.	8/8/14		To Scouts 21/1/15.
Swift, T.R.	A.	27/10/14	17/11/14	
Symes-Thompson, A.H.	B.	8/8/14	11/11/14	Lieut. 8/8/14.
Taljaard, J.	D.	7/8/14	21/1/15	To E.A.T.C.
Tannock, T.	B.	7/10/15		To E.A.S.C.
Tarlton, E.	B.	27/10/15		
Tarlton, L.	B.	8/8/14		Killed 3/11/14.
Tate, J.	B.	22/9/15		
Taylor, C.M.		5/8/14		Capt. 5/8/14; Adjutant; R.F.A.
Taylor, E.B.	C.	1/9/14	1/10/14	To Ordnance.
Taylor, F.G.	E.	25/1/15		
Taylor, F.J.	C.	28/8/14	13/1/15	
Taylor, G.	A.	8/8/14		Saddler Sergt. 20/5/15.
Taylor, H. B.	E.	15/1/15	27/4/15	From Ross's Scouts.
Theunissen, C. J.	D.	7/8/14	21/1/15	Lieut; to E.A.T.C.
Thompson, F.	B.	8/8/14		Wounded; prisoner 3/11/14.
Thompson, W. B.	B.	8/8/14	11/5/15	Sergt. 10/8/14; S.S.M. 26/9/14; to Scouts 22/10/14.
Thorne, H.	E.	15/1/15	7/6/15	Killed in action.
Thornton, F. L.	E.	29/11/15		To E.A.S.C
Thorpe, F.	B.	8/8/14		Cpl. 14/10/14; Sergt. 1/11/14.
Thrush, S.G.	E.	17/11/15		
Tillett, H.	A.	11/9/14	27/2/15	To E.A.P.C.
Todd, B.B.	B.	1/11/15		
Tomkinson, C.	C.	6/8/14	1/9/14	
Tomlinson, J.N.K.	E.		10/9/14	To E.A.S.C.

Name	Sqdn.	From	To	Remarks
Tompson, A.	A.	2/9/14	27/4/15	
Tosetti, G.	E.	11/5/15	14/9/15	
Trotter, C.J.	A.	2/9/14	27/4/15	To K.A.R.
Tryon, C.A.D.	E.	8/8/14	31/3/15	L/Cpl. 4/11/14; to E.A.S.C.
Tryon, H.C.	E.	27/2/15		Sergt. 1/3/15.
Tryon, S.	E.	25/11/14		Lieut. 25/11/14; to K.A.R.
Tunstall, W.A.	C.	6/8/14	15/3/16	To E.A. Mil. Rlys.
Tyte, J.R.	E.	20/8/15		
Ulyate, E.D.	F.	10/8/14	19/10/14	To E.A.T.C.
Ulyate, G.Z.	F.	10/8/14	19/10/14	L/Cpl. 20/8/14.
Van Aardt, P.	D.	27/8/14	21/1/15	To E.A.T.C.
Van de Heever, P.P.	D.	10/8/14	24/12/14	To E.A.T.C.
Van de Merwe, C.J.	D.	10/8/14	21/1/15	Sergt. 20/8/14; to 17th Cav.
Van de Merwe, C.S.P.	F.	10/8/14	19/10/14	L/Cpl. 20/8/14.
Van de Merwe, H.F.	D.	8/8/14	21/1/15	To E.A.T.C.
Van de Merwe, O.T.	F.	13/8/14	19/10/14	To E.A.T.C.
Van de Merwe, P.F.	D.	13/8/14	24/12/14	Wounded 3/11/14.
Van de Merwe, W.J.	D.	13/8/14	11/12/14	To E.A.T.C.
Van Deventer, C.J.	D.	27/8/14	17/11/14	
Van Niekerk, F.R.	D.	8/8/14	21/1/15	L/Cpl. 10/8/14; Cpl. 26/9/14.
Van Rensburg, J.B.	D.	8/8/14	21/1/15	To E.A.T.C.
Van Rensburg, J.C.	D.	1/9/14	21/1/15	To E.A.T.C.
Van Rensburg, L.W.	D.	1/9/14	21/1/15	To E.A.T.C.
Van Vunren, C.J.	D.	8/8/14	21/1/15	To E.A.T.C.
Vetter, H.E.	M.G.S.	8/9/14		To K.A.R.
Viljoen, J.J.	D.	7/8/14	21/1/15	Cpl. 10/8/14; Sergt. 26/ 9/14; S.S.M. 1/12/14; to E.A.T.C.
Viljoen, S.	D.	27/8/14	17/12/14	
Vincent, F.R.	C.	19/9/14		
Vogelzang, H.J.	E.	12/2/15		
Wahl, D.	D.	9/8/14	21/1/15	To E.A.T.C.
Walker, E.	A.	7/8/14	27/4/15	To K.A.R.
Walker, F.H.	A.	8/11/15		
Walker, J.A.	E.	7/10/15		
Walker, W.	C.	25/1/15		
Wangenberg, N.T.	B.	13/8/14	2/3/15	Re-enlisted 7/9/15.
Warberg, J.I.	A.	14/9/15		
Ware, C.W.	A.	14/8/14	12/11/14	To Ordnance.
Ward, C.W.	C.		3/11/14	
Warwick, N.R.C.	E.	26/11/14	27/ 4/15	To E.A.S.C.
Watcham, S.D.		20/3/16		
Watkins, H.G.	B.-C.	8/8/14		L/Cpl. 10/8/14.
Watson, B.	M.G.S.	8/8/14	27/4/15	
Wearing, E.C.	E.	6/12/15		
Webb, B.F.	E.	8/8/14		Lieut. 10/8/14; Capt. 9/11/14; wounded 3/11/14; to K.A.R.
Webb, K.McD.	E.	7/10/15		
Webb, S.R.	E.	7/10/15		
Webber, W.H.	C.	2/9/14		Cpl. 9/11/15; awarded D.C.M; to K.A.R.
Weinholt, A.				Scouts.
Weir, W.V.	E.	23/4/15		To E.A.S.C.
Weller, F.H.	A.	8/11/15		
Wells, H.T.	A.	11/9/14	7/1/15	
Wheeler, R.C.				Capt. E.A.V.C. Atchd.
Wheelock, P.	A.	10/8/14	26/10/14	To 2nd L. of D.
White, E.D.A.	B.	8/8/14	26/8/14	
Whitehead, A.	E.	8/8/14	2/10/14	

Name	Sqdn.	From	To	Remarks
Whittingham, O.H.	E.	18/9/14		
Wilbraham, C.H.	B.-C.	8/8/14		
Wilbourne, A.K.	C.	6/3/15		To Signals 1/6/15.
Wild, F.J.	B.	12/10/15		
Wiley, G.C.	A.	7/8/14		L/Cpl. 2/9/14; Sergt. 26/1/15; Lieut. 6/12/15; To Administration.
Wilkes, B.C.	C.	26/8/14	1/5/15	To I.D.
Wilkinson, M.H.	E.	15/1/15		
Wilkinson, N.H.	C.	7/8/14	10/11/14	To Ross's Scouts.
Willey, V.A.	E.	27/1/15		
Wiliams, A.S.	C.	8/8/14		L/Cpl. 19/8/15; to Scouts 14/10/15; to K.A.R.
Willoughby, B.	B.	8/8/14	19/11/14	
Willoughby, J.	B.	8/8/14	19/11/14	
Wison, C.J.				Capt. E.A.M.S.; M.O. Attchd.
Wilson, F. O'B.	Scouts	1/11/14		From Magadi Defence Force; Capt 3/11/14.
Wison, J.J.	E.	8/8/14	11/2/15	Sergt. 10/8/14; to M.L.C.
Wilson, J.J.V.	E.	8/8/14	26/11/14	L/Cpl. 8/10/14.
Wilson, R.G.H.	C.	1/12/14		To K.A.R.
Wison, R.H.	A.		28/8/14	Sergt. 10/ 8/14; to 2nd L. of D.
Windinge, C.V.S.	E.	15/9/14	18/11/14	
Winter, J.V.	C.	25/11/15		
Wisdom, L.A.	C.	9/9/14		
Woolman, A.	E.	8/8/14	21/12/14	
Wood, G.A.	C.	6/3/15		
Wood, H.K.	A.	6/12/15		To K.A.R.
Woodgate, H.P.	B.	8/8/14	4/12/14	To Signals 22/9/14; to Loyal N. Lancs.
Woods, W.J.	E.	7/10/15		
Wood, W.	A.	30/10/15		
Wright, C.C. de V.	C.	13/8/14	23/10/14	Wounded 25/9/14; to K.A.R.
Wroth, W.A.	A.	4/10/15		
Young, C.E.	C.	6/8/14	26/6/15	
Young, J.W.	E.	10/9/14	27/4/15	
Zimmerman, H.P.	C.	10/2/15		To M.L.C.

LEONAUR

ALSO FROM LEONAUR
AVAILABLE IN SOFTCOVER OR HARDCOVER WITH DUST JACKET

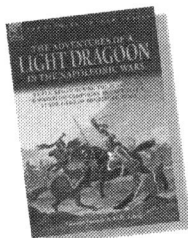

EW12 EYEWITNESS TO WAR SERIES
THE ADVENTURES OF A LIGHT DRAGOON IN THE NAPOLEONIC WARS
by George Farmer & G.R. Gleig

A Cavalryman During the Peninsular & Waterloo Campaigns, in Captivity & at the Seige of Bhurtpore, India.

SOFTCOVER : **ISBN 1-84677-040-8**
HARDCOVER : **ISBN 1-84677-056-4**

MC2 THE MILITARY COMMANDER SERIES
THE RECOLLECTIONS OF SKINNER OF SKINNERS HORSE
by James Skinner

James Skinner & His 'Yellow Boys' Irregular Cavalry in the Wars of India Between the British, Mahratta, Rajput, Mogul, Sikh & Pindarree Forces.

SOFTCOVER : **ISBN 1-84677-061-0**
HARDCOVER : **ISBN 1-84677-071-8**

EW13 EYEWITNESS TO WAR SERIES
THE RED DRAGOON
by W.J. Adams

With the 7th Dragoon Guards in the Cape of Good Hope Against the Boers and the Kaffir Tribes During the 'War of the Axe' 1843-48.

SOFTCOVER : **ISBN 1-84677-043-2**
HARDCOVER : **ISBN 1-84677-057-2**

EW14 EYEWITNESS TO WAR SERIES
ZULU 1879
Selected by D.C.F. Moodie & the Leonaur Editors

The Anglo-Zulu War of 1879 from Contemporary Sources; First Hand Accounts, Interviews, Dispatches, Official Documents & Newspaper Reports.

SOFTCOVER : **ISBN 1-84677-044-0**
HARDCOVER : **ISBN 1-84677-051-3**

AVAILABLE ONLINE AT
www.leonaur.com
AND OTHER GOOD BOOK STORES

LEONAUR

www.ingramcontent.com/pod-product-compliance
Lightning Source LLC
Chambersburg PA
CBHW021112090426

42738CB00006B/616